Exercises in Romantic Understanding

Andrew Franck

Archetextural

archetextural@gmail.com

Arts • Media • Books

W o o d s t o c k , N Y

Exercises In Romantic Understanding
© 2016 Andrew Franck
ISBN-10: 1519385579
ISBN-13: 978-1519385574
Published by ARCHETEXTURAL
All Right Reserved

He who knows the virtue of the dance lives in God because he knows how love slays.

-Rumi

Introduction: The Urge To Reinvent Sensibility

Given the possibilities, desire unsheathes perpetual reinventions of sensibility. The many ingenious strains borne on attraction characterize the conviction that yearning guides destiny toward loftier goals; that feeling enables the soul to craft a new and potentially exceptional reality. Respiring through feeling, desire insistently draws attention to the object of affection. With a self-propelled impulse, expectation increases an emotive mix of allure and ardor. Reserved or flaunted, like a gentle summer breeze or a raging blaze, romance sets the air on fire. The world's trajectory seems to operate more triumphal when, ignited, we're cast into its central role.

Romance is a complicated term with a complicated history. Ancient Greek tragedy already harbored proto-romantic characteristics such as the story of Theseus, the founder-king of Athens who slays the Minotaur with the help of his starry-eyed accomplice-lover, Ariadne. Following Ariadne's bestowal of a sword and ball of string to aid the hero's fight and safe return from the maze, she and Theseus are ultimately led to estrangement by the goddesses Ananke and Moiria; the goddesses enact forces of necessity and fate, upholding Ariadne's predestined marriage to the god Dionysus. In Homer's *Odyssey* the contextual lure for the distant beloved establishes through the magnetizing force between the patiently waiting wife, Penelope, and the adventurer-hero Ulysses, who must overcome the nigh impossible before his return home. In the Middle Ages, the illicit love affair between the theologian Peter Abelard and the innovative scholar Héloïse is disclosed through their prolific love letters. Filled with philosophic acumen and a passionate heart, Heloise candidly writes, "I preferred love to wedlock, freedom to a bond." Her exceptional love for Peter illustrates her emancipation from church dogma and social custom. Again, tragedy reigns when their lives are set asunder by misunderstandings and prescribed moral impositions. From the courtly love of Mallory's *Morte d'Arthur* including the romances of Lancelot and Guinevere, Tristan and Isolde, to Cervantes' *Don Quixote*, we encounter the romantic themes of chivalry and amatory chase as a theater of poetry, lure, and adventure. Perhaps nowhere else is the emotive force of romance led to higher reflection than in *Roman de la Rose*, the medieval French poetic masterpiece of courtly love that asserts with the celebrated line "a man who

1

does not experience love cannot picture it," a common maxim variously quoted from the troubadours to Dante's *Vita Nuova*. The *"Donna me prega,"* Guido Calvacanti's remarkable *canzone* on the anatomy of love, addresses love as it is embodied sensually: its origins, faculties, and virtues, its power and essence, and what actually permits it to *be love*. The importance of Cavalcanti's verse is its ability to describe what goes on in the poet/lover's mind in a detailed, personal manner, establishing sensuous, autobiographic poetry. A revolution regarding love and its romantic implications was born.

Overall, as the idea of romantic pursuit gained shape, its agents commonly detach mentality from a host of practical issues. The quest inclines into a private sphere openly establishing an atmosphere of *otherness* toward the world. Not typically arising from the lovers' own urge for close examination, the emotionally charged context of romance clearly steers away from cognizing an escalating self-involvement; ostensibly, the romantic quest is a corrective for the faltering mundanity all around; it's an exalted variety of existence from which the "sensible" majority appears estranged. Subliminally demoting social and utilitarian affairs to intrusions looming beneath a newly-valued horizon, romantic imagination gathers up exploratory quality, striking out to impress, please and evolve the liaison, often subordinating responsibilities and duties into categories of lesser concern. Romantic imagination devotes itself to a "higher" cause: love. Or what love is believed to be. Expressing romantic feeling declares solidarity through a wish to establish togetherness, closeness, to become more intimate through shared secrets. And often, lust. Romance can upset routines, destroy good sense, and disrupt the wholesome initiative with which it started out. How the risk of romance is played against wellbeing, how longing unfolds, how the future is invented and amplified can launch passion toward a brink. Romance can be a perilous journey heedless of security and composure. Besides, there is *love* that makes the whole situation feel complete, unless or until what seems to be love gives way to provinces of foolishness or madness.

Social conventions clearly have a vested interest in formatting attraction, acknowledging romance's idealized versions of passionate enthusiasm while at the same time attempting to appropriate its exclusionary impulse, its untamed tendencies. The collective ethos aims to, in the end, steer attraction toward the normalcy of the common welfare. Usually, from the lovers' point of view, this attitude isn't reciprocated. Given that affection involutes into exceptional proclivities and endless searching for erotic completion, prevailing social attitudes are felt to be least inclined for comprehending inner urges. Regarding potential disquiet and consequences, cultural wellbeing may be of little concern for lovers. As Emerson noted, "The heart has arguments with which the understanding is not acquainted." Along with friendship, loyalty, trust, and honor, the heart braves desire, passion, and sexual appetite. How do those who are unstirred comprehend this drive? Since the time of ancient China, Persia, India, and Greece, culture sets out to demonstrably consider and deal with the fascination of amorousness and romance. Accordingly, to be sensible means to believe that these impulses eventually mature, that life itself leads to assuaging the intrigues of the passionately stricken heart. Keenly aware of the longing of those souls seeking exclusivity, the social ethos curbs the venturesome impulses of fantasy and fascination through protocols of ritual and institutions. Establishing conventions for upholding good sense, passion is directed toward an integrated normalcy. Marriage, family, work, and civic obligation are the customary means. These attempts to guide passion—striving to mitigate the effects of longing—usher in far-ranging effects, some successful, others not so much. Encouraged by romance, new bonds, kinships, and conflicts sculpt community with novel influences, the consequence of interwoven ideologies and proclivities. This is particularly evident through the mingling of cultures; the fusion expressed through language, music, arts and cuisine often yields surprising results.

Another sort of appreciation emerged during the historically designated Romantic era when the fruits of the Enlightenment felt an impulse to stir hearts in artistic, imagination-laden ways. Romanticism, a movement prizing intuition and emotion over rationalism, began as a stirring force in eighteenth century Germany, England, and France. Romanticism elevated the achievements of individualists and artists whose pioneering efforts aspired to uplift the ordinary. It also legitimized the personalized imagination as a critical authority, enabling independence from classical notions of form, especially in the arts, and relationships. According to Humphry Davy, a prominent Romantic thinker, poet and scientist, Romanticism required "an attitude of admiration, love and worship… a personal response." The music of Chopin, Schumann, and List, the poetry of Novalis, Blake, and Coleridge, the paintings of Delacroix, Corot, Goya, Runge, and Turner are a few examples of the romantic drive meeting the emotional character of their time. Romance had found social and artistic legitimacy through recognizing the creative force in reinventing sensibility. Romanticism acknowledged above all the inner life, declaring everything that springs from this inner life as valuable. Given this notion of living wholly through the upwelling of the self, Romanticism wished to render the world as a realm of artistic impulse, creation through free imaginative power rising above everything that determines an individual from the outside world, rising above a normative moral order. In its urge regarding self-direction and excitement, Romantic morality portrays chiefly an esthetic morality founded upon on the worth of imagination and of the unrestrained powers of the soul; these form a conception by which man appears as perfect and as free as possible. Awe, terror, apprehension and reverie achieved a firm footing within this psyche. With the Romantics arose a deep reflection: how to have religious experience without necessarily engaging in formal religious practices. For them, normative religion held the world in a kind of stasis, flattened, and regressive. More than a few Romantics had some understanding of the ancient mystery initiations: of being delivered into a theogenic world, a god-generated process, a search not for an external God but for a self-delivering, intra-human divinity. That said, perhaps the most discerning of how the richness of soul, feeling life, and the element of love spread throughout individualized imagination arrives through the poet Novalis. Novalis understood the self-conscious soul as being rooted in spiritual experience; its origins are not established in the world of the senses. He feels and experiences himself as having his being founded in a higher spiritual nature, expressing this as one who "lifts the veil of the goddess…[and sees]…himself." This lifting of the goddess' or god's veil was destined to have a remarkably unconscious yet deeply profound power within the romantic psyche and its ongoing influence.

Many a romantic felt nature, the elements, storms, the mood of the times each as the workings of the imagination of divine beings. Though mostly trivialized in present-day culture, the spiritually amorous approach—the point of romance in very palpable ways—laid the foundation for modern spiritual experience. Self-realized divinity's motifs, according to William Blake, surface by way of the Imagination. Every being evolves from creature to creator through imagination; but it is the quality and character of the creative act, the quality and character of the Imagination itself that is divine. Imagination however needs to be cultivated; the god-like capacity within all human beings *is* the creative imagination en route to the deific. Differentiating imagination and Imagination, William Blake understood Imagination as " the body of God." For Blake, "Energy is eternal delight."

Romantic sensibility and sentiment especially intensified through the development of Western literature. Already in Shakespeare's sonnets and his tragedy of Romeo and Juliet are typified the heartfelt urges that seek the beloved in the most hopeless of circumstances. Later, the romance novel begun by such notables as Samuel Richardson and Jane Austin eventually led to romance's literary themes becoming a genre. In Gothic novels such as Bram Stroker's *Dracula* the elements of yearning and romantic seduction descend into forbidden forces mingled with fear and dread; the generative potency of passion becomes seized by the dark impulses of obsession and everlasting longing. Looking even further back, antecedent to the romance novel can be found as far back as ancient Egypt, China and Rome. We know it today as the love letter. The philosophically probing yet passionate letters of Abelard and Heloise are classic examples of how yearning unfolds between lovers. Their very words carry a deeply poignant thrust. A love letter acts to expound emotion, to ease or amplify yearning. To lay bare the soul.

Declaring deep emotion can, as well, set in motion more of what's *not* stated than what is. At times, the love letter can be preferable to face-to-face contact given that thoughts, in addition to being composed, reviewed, and revised, may be expounded to allow feelings a greater expression than if the writer were in the beloved's presence. Proclaiming devotion, disappointment, self-confidence, ambition, or impatience places the beloved in a position of confidante and muse. Further, through the textual expression of ardent feelings, emotions gain strength through declarations of desire. Written words restate the significance and worth of the beloved and the writer's attention to the beloved's presence. The personal thrill of receiving a love note serves to emphasize the importance of how passion is unfettered by spatial separation. New insights may surface. Enticement flirts with relief; the comedy of seduction provokes hilarity. New feelings or new disappointments may direct the intensity of fervent flow. Romantic love releases a spectrum of discourse and intercourse, words and gestures as formidable forces for intimacy. Love is fierce and tender, complex and difficult. We come to learn how love itself elevates and refines when stating a clear, passionate intent to become expressive. Love changes one's own experience as one learns that personal aptitude regarding romance is only a steppingstone toward embracing the other.

Attempting to Navigate Romantic Sensibility

Generally, an exercise is designed to develop skill, support and articulate an emerging faculty, embellish and advance know-how. One gets a clearer understanding of the subject by relating more deeply through dedicated training. Through intention and qualified pursuit, practice has a goal. To systematically pursue a goal assumes maintaining discipline. The eventual fruits of the endeavor allow for more confidence, expectantly, and understanding. When commencing dance lessons or attempting a scientific experiment, there are methods available for directing or guiding the process. An unfaultable method would constitute a set of stages each following the other, each unambiguous in intent. The most orderly method would be one where the steady executing of skill makes no demand for inner changes in the participant. On the other hand, a method that embraces disciplining one's character requires controlled behavior, the obliging *of* one's core, the building of fortitude while attenuating shortcomings. This discipline necessitates change of the inner life. One can see how a method may sidetrack from a deeper understanding if its approach gets stuck in routine and theory. Discipline means to keep focus intact. The fundamental attitude of discipline is grounded *in the body*, growing alert to variations and unusual conditions; a state not usually examined by those involved in a burgeoning romance. All things considered, in science, medicine, and technology, method and discipline are necessarily closely knit. In education and the arts they can springboard from one to the other, often with satisfying results. In romance however, practical discipline inheres through concern, proposition, fantasy, and elucidation; discipline in this setting may lead to the relationship itself surfacing as a "work of art." With a love note the *negative space* implied by patience and the wait for a response is expected; method is categorically transparent and duly ruled out.

Romantic results require communicating heartfelt wishes. Concealed in the background is the notion that being aware of thought itself derives from erotic dialogue. Plato himself remarked that only the lover is "full of god." Thus, through love letters, promises of fulfillment provoke the beloved toward greater significance, paradoxically enabling power over another's soul while inadvertently rallying the self to abandon reason. The love letter increases romance by "sacrificially" stretching the membrane of oneself toward the other by way of attention, or being pulled by seduction. Bound closely by feeling, lovers appear more liberated. Appearing free, strategies ensue. To understand romance, a lover needs to exercise discipline in his or her devotion, effectively keeping one's head through expressive abandon. And in common parlance, those who are passionate can *get better* with this practice.

In contrast, engaging in a romantic endeavor may have the misfortune of bringing about adverse results. If a relationship goes into a tailspin, each one involved can be convinced of their singular correctness, or grow skilled at maintaining their own position so that continuing the relationship becomes an exercise in futility. If the bond ultimately fails, returning love letters or burning them affirms something deeply painful, tacitly memorializing a future that couldn't be realized. Stunned, one has discovered confidences, moods and boundaries capable of being breached by another who once engaged intimately into loving connection. Like with Goethe's sensitive letter-writing Werther, who tortures himself due to unrequited love, the feeling of abyss provides little hope or insight, ultimately leading to suicide. Goethe himself, who was grief-stricken by the failure of his own love obsession, was to later denounce the Romantic Movement as "everything that is sick." That said, considering certain moods regarding commitment, the ache of what was once regarded as precious and exclusionary (or what leads to that which imposes on personal autonomy) can be addressed by the conscious awareness of the value of commitment itself. Despite residual guilt, pain and regrets, in recognizing how elevating impulse and fantasy languished into method rather than urged into a discipline for "completing" oneself, the failure of romance *can* mature romantic understanding. Whatever emotion is invested in another human being cannot diminish the value of what it *meant to* invest in that other human being. Cognizing the worth of this reveals evolvement of character. And through the course of character-making the deeper gifts of romance can more readily be revealed.

Hazarding A Fulcrum: Intent, Desire, Fate and Will

The metaphysics of love cultivates in the varieties of separation. Even if bidding to exhaust itself, the soul harbors desire, seeks attachment, "completion." Some of the soul's drives may be impulsive, relentless, uncompromising. Forbidden or hysterical urges can occupy a soul's nature; infatuation, even possession—an intense captivity through attraction—takes up spiritual-somatic residence. Building momentum, certain romantic drives aim to exalt beauty, otherness, mystery. However, if the soul is convinced that a relationship incline in a prescribed manner, the world can appear fixated, "explained;" the familiar feels overly reinforced, concluded, conceivably spent through its achievements. Having dissipated the forces of attraction, what was imagined to be love may then rear monstrously as a response to being "let down," shifted away from the intensity of yearning's impulse. Or if grown aloof, the soul might respond with chilled reasoning: how can the cosmos, let alone lovers, endure much of this emotive distraction? The dualities within which the soul exists and is inexorably drawn to requires another power balancing passion and reason, poising attraction and love, self and other. Ignoring this balancing power, not a few of the Romantics ended up tragically exhausted or worse. Yet with well-crafted and supported feeling of what can be offered *to* attraction, love is prepared to offer its gift regarding what the wisdom within attraction may be.

• • •

A fluky boarding reassignment led the ensuing chronicle's lovers to meet. Already far in advance of this encounter, she felt pursued by a secret longing from just this sort of man. Quietly settling into the adjoining seat, he elects to avoid even a hint of banter; he'd rather not come off like most men who'd jump at the opportunity to engage such a stunningly attractive woman. His seeming indifference leads her to quietly reflect on the thrill she now feels filling her soul, and the meaning of desire she's mused upon practically forever. Her lips begin to tingle. Her fingers tremble. As the plane readies on the runway, she dares herself, and concocts a not altogether innocent ploy. Turning toward him, she asks if he'd hold her hand for a moment; she's sometimes scared of taking off, she says softly, almost shuddering. At cruising altitude, she finally lets go. It's only an hour and a bit in the air but in that interval he learns that she lives in Albuquerque; she teaches grade school, is married and unhappily devoted to keeping her nuptial vows. He listens silently till prompted. He mentions but a few things about himself, yet she's intrigued by it all. Ready to part upon landing, they exchange addresses. If she finds herself sometime in the Northeast, they should consider having tea, he says. Their goodbyes are with the eyes of souls that already wish to be kissing. Consumed, she writes to him within a week. And he replies. They quickly find that each imagines love itself providing the storehouse of their destiny. And, as love's *will* grows more accessible, they discover how their longing must take into account a store of concerns and consequences. Likewise, they realize that a journey of elation, heartbreak, and self-examination has just begun. Their dilemmas stand on waves of promise and transfiguration while harboring the supposition that love somehow establishes a unique spiritual horizon through the course of their romance; that love awakens from a story that warrants articulation owing to some beacon of necessity. Through storylines they imagine the force of erotic desire and potency unveiling through their present lives. Independently, they reflect: How is it that we believe we can *give* love? Toward *what* does love truly propel? How is it that an imagination of *pleasuring* the other seems to inform one's connection to life? Expressed, established and complicated through written correspondences, the extent of their shaky circumstance sequesters the "real" world, yet its shadows are convened and dismissed by their shared passion. Spatial and temporal curbs are met by quixotic reveries further launching their mystical quest. But by refracting their identities, implicating the astonishing force within attraction, their depth of intimacy increases. Devoted through their pining, they both admit and refuse failures of love, unlocking a dimension that unescapably turns longing inside out, a mirror gazing back to its endless source through portals of discovery. Is this the manner of engaging the philosophy of love? Straining expectation and results, they become each other's thread, a thread on which love is strung, revealing who and what hadn't been whole, fulfilled, or capable of gathering the majesty of their ache.

Aspiring to fathom the efforts of romance, they, by way of these "exercises," explore an unfolding resonance, one that exalts their participation within the aims of yearning.

Part 1

Q B S P

Que Besa Su Pes

"Who Kisses Your Feet"

(formal close in Spanish letters)

28 Aug

I had no intention of writing to you after we cordially exchanged addresses; a kind of "formality" given a serendipitous conversation with a stranger on a plane. No, I was impelled. Mornings, on my way to work, I keep musing of you having your cup of tea with your bees. "Breakfast with the girls," as you put it. You're just there, in my thoughts.

Re-iterating what I mentioned: I believe the divine is very much separate from me, my world. Being a part of the universe is so much an unfulfilled promise, like Eden's serpent luring toward existence here, consciously, then delivering the goods. Consciousness as punishment? Everything remains more estranged than ever; primordial absorption into a persistent unknown.

I wonder to which school run by Dominicans you went. Are your memories of them as unpleasant as mine? Just for the record, it's my response to those very nuns that I attribute my peculiar penmanship.

Hoping you're well,

Faye

I had no intention of writing to you after we exchanged addresses just days ago. But sometimes, now, in the morning, I think of you having tea with your bees... breakfast with the girls as you put it, and I turn over in bed smiling. Today I didn't bother getting up. Or did I? (I must've since I'm at work.)

On that day, our first meeting, I told you, and perhaps this is unfortunate for me, that for me God and I are so separate from one another that it makes me cry. Today is a day I must cry: the primordial scraps I feel borne through some long ago forbidden fruit are disjunctions the world must compellingly tread.

Remember when you mentioned that business about personality taking itself too literally, too real? I wonder that about everything now, even about the words I'm now writing. By the way, I attribute my penmanship to those very nuns schooling me towards perfection. It's from their idea of perfection I've in fact been running ever since.

Please tell me about your Dominicans; my school days shouldn't still gnaw at me at this point.

All best,

Faye

This letter has taken so long to construct. I've written at least a hundred notes since receiving yours, though this is the first on paper. Your saga at Sacred Heart sounds as though you endured a very real "cloud of unknowing." Then, even with all that, you headed for the seminary. I feel as though I can understand what you meant about questing for transcendence. I went to John the Evangelist till grade six and still feel pummeled.

Marla (my dearest friend and cat) is reading this over my arm. She thinks you're very crazy, especially when I laughed aloud after you wrote about you being a cosmogonic virgin. Remember that that long-ago Harmonic Convergence, which didn't seem to change anything as far as anyone I know can tell? The whole thing still makes me smile. Oh, I might be wrong: you're likely not an occultist though I sense how secretive you are.

I'm sorry I revealed to you certain things that I'm not very proud of. Especially at our first meeting, no less. I don't know what possessed me. Something deeply inside needed to bare my soul to you. God knows why. Maybe that was my rendering of what confession ought to be. Reading people is both a blessing and a curse; seeing too much, and often too soon.

Wishing you the best,

Faye

Forget everything I said about wishes being like horses. If they were, I'd be well on my way to L'Étoile du Nord, Star of the North right now, the place of my birth, which, no matter how cold it gets, it ' a comforting womb to me.

Now that I've accepted a full-time teaching position everyone says I've done the right thing. Even my husband's parents believe it's the right thing. To keep me "out of trouble" is what I believe they think. Even after eight years of me being their daughter in law, they can't (or won't) spell my name correctly. Yet they dredge up the time I broke their son's heart whenever they can. We'd been married for three years, and since day two I thought it best to leave; being together was wrong from the start. I felt my soul being ignored, completely; enough so that when someone came along who I believed *knew* something, who felt the world, who desperately wanted me, I ran to him. Into the fire from the frying pan it turned out. It was all about the charm I soon found out. I've had to pay ever since, and I do by being a dutiful wife, not the spoiled brat as some suggest. I tell myself that I vowed "forever" at the altar and some demon (or is it my conscience?) makes me continue to stay. I keep asking: how is genuine marriage possible?

Perhaps someday I'll transcend both the brat *and* the reluctant wife in me. Perhaps I'll one day resolve this battle and go live alone. I hate to spew out these yearning pains to you.

Faye

P.S. Speaking of synchronicities, the day we met, my assigned seat on the plane was several rows behind yours. That was changed unexpectedly at the last minute; the gate agent said it was necessary. Necessary? Yes, necessary. I'd like to thank him for that. I hate to think how easily I almost missed meeting you.

Thomas Eakins met his wife in a painting class and their marriage lasted their lifetimes. As did their devotion to each other. Just lucky? Or was it meant to be? An extraordinary bond through art that held them together? Or something even deeper?

I can understand the Shakers vow of celibacy, helping to simplify their spiritual intent. Sex complicates and often confuses the whole lot. In this overly acquisitive and self-seeking world sex can become the sole sacrament. Even with the enormous disjunction between sex and love, in nature all that seems unified and guided by instinct. Seems like what the animal world *doesn't* know makes it all the more wholesome.

I seem to have given up on wanting to have children. It breaks my heart when I see children brought up with so little wisdom penetrating their daily lives. On the other hand, is it that I'd love to have children? That it would be the sweetest gift. If I sound confused, I am.

But just this: do you have a family, a lover, a wife? Are you cherished? Are you happy? You've hardly told me anything about yourself. Please?

Until soon,

Faye

When I read your second letter a voice at the edge of daydream said, "this can't be real." Then another voice said, "This makes all the sense in the world." I'm not sure about anything at the moment. I feel after so long the difficulty of finding words to articulate the hidden part within me. I find a quiet place in myself through writing you.

I wish I could quit this charade; it's more than painful. My heart, as you suggested, is feeling many shadows; it lives among them. Everything becomes diffused, escaping me through a sieve of my own devices. Then somehow I breathe a wholesome sigh of relief when thinking of you. I feel as "one soul in two bodies" just thinking of you.

The universe allows for us making mistakes, no? But why do I find having *this* kind of conscience so hard to bear? When you mentioned the struggle it takes to feel the world as one's dwelling did you imply that you yourself do? I've known quite a few uncomfortable "homes."

Faye

Why was I always *becoming* ready for what *had* to happen? Becoming ready for meeting you? Intimacy always seemed to require my *perceiving* the past, my incarnation like a dying particle, a part depositing a phylogenetic trace. Echoes of wishes becoming possibilities. From those rumors arose this body generating its stories seeking the breadth, the questions, the replies of another. That other, you, is the force, the splendid vacuum that's been pulling me to myself long before I had any awareness of what heaven may be drawing me into. On the wide screen, I caused a scandal to move closer to a fairy tale.

Marla brought in a very large black, white and red bird to the door. In her mouth. After being rescued, the bird just looked into my eyes in a very beautiful, sad sort of way. Then let out a doleful squawk as if to make peace with death. Just when I thought the little creature was ready to collapse it suddenly upped and flew off! I can't help feeling the bird was brought in not by chance. Was it fate? Magic? An omen?

Maybe I now understand what you mean when you mention *expansion* and *contraction* in the "dream elixir." As movement made visible, they illustrate moments "at Midday, Midnight, Twilight and Dawn when the river can be crossed the other way, back from the sense-perceptible world to Spirit Land."

With love,

Faye

You're wonderful and crazy sending me that huge box of autumn leaves: maples, oaks, poplar and ash! I'm totally drunk with them. Yay, what fun! I'm going to dump them in the middle of the living room and jump into the whole pile!

Do you remember during that brief first time we met when I told you that my marriage is like some unstated agreement to feel less and more, in inappropriate proportions? As if the superficial engages the immediacy of the present in a way that feeling deeper does not. How can a connection with someone go awry? Lost. None of it deeply makes sense. To complicate things, there seems to be many kinds of love, degrees of loving.

Why is it that all my relationships end up with me being lonelier with someone than without? It perplexes me. Heaven forgive me for dreaming about you being different.

And about those leaves,
thank you, forever

Faye

P.S. My birthday (the real one that is) is May 1st. You still haven't told me yours and I'm not a very patient person.

In case you didn't receive the letter that I sent to Stuttgart, thank you so so much for my gift. No one has ever given me anything as wonderful as a cartload of leaves thru the mail. Something I'll treasure always and forever.

When you mentioned prescribed morality, isn't that religion's aim? What about those spirits in the Bible who said, "Let us make men in our image, after our likeness." My question is: in whose image and likeness? Who are they who said it? What is "their image and likeness"? If the Elohim created humanity in their image and likeness then why would they wish to urge an apparently perfect image and likeness *to be*, or to be something other than who they are? Or to create just because they could? I mean, even if through the wile of the serpent, wouldn't the fruit of knowledge be all the more warranted to save humanity from all its impending ridiculousness? Does any of what "image and likeness" purport seem like a misrepresentation of their and our place in the Cosmos?

Anyway, I'm not sure how you'll take this I'm sending you my Saint Christopher medallion—*Christo phoros*, the carrier of Christ. For me, it's important that you have it.

Faye

I'm not as glum as my last note would make things seem. Impatient, yes. Maybe I'll distract myself by painting some cows on the side of the house. Cows are, for me, even more peaceful than Buddha. Except maybe the Devil's Herd — a very mean bunch of black Brangus kept by a farmer down the road. They are *not* very cow-like.

Mentioning Buddha, I often think about the four noble truths elucidated by Siddhartha in his first talk after his great awakening. All these right thoughts, actions, deeds: it's about the self's orientation, regardless of whether or not there is a self. I'm sure that I have a self. Though not so sure the self is me.

Faye

P.S. How sweet you are to surprise your mother on her birthday, flying back early from Germany. I bet she loved seeing you! Mostly, I'm happy to know that you *do* have a mother. I had almost begun thinking that you grew up in some God-forsaken Catholic orphanage.

Last night I dreamt of dancing around a fire. It's a dream I have repeatedly. Then, this morning I found three cat whiskers. I took both events to be an auspicious sign. Your dream elixir is starting to work.

I'm in the middle of packing, getting ready to pack for my annual visit to Mexico. Every year I visit the Basilica of the Virgin of Zapopan with its image of the Virgin Mary. The statue there was first crafted in Michoacán by artisans in the 16th century. It's quite small, set on the altar and made with corn stalks except for her hands, which are made of wood. The locals also call her Our Lady of Expectation, proclaiming her their Patroness against storms and lightning ever since centuries ago. They say she brought an end to the Mixtón War in the 16th century, and relief from epidemics that plagued Guadalajara in the 17th century. But it's not for the art or history or healing I go. Face to face, I absorb her gentle countenance, her gesture of balancing on a crescent Moon, her unpretentious splendor. She seems to embody what I most dearly wish for, and what I might be capable of giving someone I truly love.

Two years ago I left my husband for another man, someone even less of what was essential. The affair was very short-lived and I returned, horrible as that all was. My husband's a good person. He's happy with himself and his work. It has always hurt to know how much he loves me. And I do need to be loved. But—and this has always been the strangest of things for me— this love between us has always harbored an absence within it. A gulf looming, based upon how contrived a relationship really is when established solely on attraction. Or comfort. Some imperative compels me to stay. To stay as if in some significant way not to betray whatever the love he has for me, though I can hardly to bear it. What does someone do with all this indecision? I can't morally imagine leaving him again. But I can't honestly imagine staying.

Fondly,

The Reigning Queen of Transfixion

P.S. *There exists two kinds of rapture one of which arises from human illness and the other from divine exaltation, whereby we feel ourselves to be extraneous to normal laws or customs.* — Plato, *Phaedrus*

Your writing me about Santa Lucia had me imagine an altogether mystical, resplendent realm. I would've loved to be there and hear those middle of the night voices that you heard. And, I would love for you to come to Taos Pueblo with me for Christmas Eve vespers and dances. And midnight Mass. Complete with hundreds of luminarias on all the rooftops. You're as crazy as I am about magical things. Have you ever been to the White Dove of the Desert? If so, during a time with snow on the Saguaros?

Have a lovely Christmas.

Faye

I almost called you but then I realized you must've left for the holiday. But, talking to you might make you seem more real than your letters. I'm not sure I'm ready for that.

Faye

P.S. Whoever said "love is the triumph of imagination over intelligence" definitely got under my Christmas tree.

Now that I know you unpacked your package you have real New Mexican luminarias. Don't forget to fold down the sides once or twice and put sand in the bottoms so they don't tip and catch fire. And also - this is my own tradition - make a wish with each one you light.

Until your letter arrived it seemed like forever since I'd heard from you. I've missed you, which seems strange given the short time we've existed as friends (today is five months since we met). I refuse to think that I may never see you again. There can never be too much of what makes happiness. And that's what thinking of you is to me.

I am very much in the mood to share a secret thing with you, one that I've always known would happen. I've known this every moment since being a kid. But the secret thing I wanted to share with you I realize now is terribly private and romantic and I find myself unable to tell it until you're ready to share a secret with me.

With much love.

Fayte

P.S. Please, please, please tell me when your birthday is. If you don't I swear I'll never write to you again.

Dearest One

"If I had a single flower for every time I think of you I would walk forever in my garden."

Please, oh please be my valentine

(I miss you more than I ever thought possible.)

P.S.

WHY WE NEED PASSION IN OUR LIVES

"Passion plays a central and organizing function in our lives," says Carl Goldberg, Ph.D., associate clinical professor of psychiatry at Albert Einstein College of Medicine in NYC. Passion - whether it's romantic and sexual or an idealistic drive to improve our lives or the world - invigorates us, inspires us, and defines our goals. When people have nothing to long for, Goldberg claims, their days become fragmented and aimless.

Goldberg believes that passion today is in trouble, that too many people try to analyze it away as being unreal, unworthy, or impulsive. This cynical view stems, he believes, from Freud's bias against romantic love. "Freud mistrusted sexual passion as a binding force in a mature relationship," Goldberg says. Freud regarded the desire for romantic love as a "magical wish," a result of repressed childhood love for the parent. For Freud, the healthy adult solution was sublimation into altruistic and artistic pursuits.

But this notion, Goldberg believes, has had devastating, unintentional effects: "Psychological inquiry, which originally sought to free us from the bonds of repressed motives, has come full circle" -- making the modern person a prisoner of her own introspective search. She becomes, Goldberg adds, "less concerned with what she is directly experiencing with others than with what she infers or seeks to find as the 'real' reason or motive behind her attractions." When people regard passion as "displaced" or "inappropriate," they devalue their own feelings and convictions. The sad result, says Goldberg, is that "a kiss that should taste delectably sweet is denied its flavor, a caress its tender touch, a smile its assurance."

As misguided as I think Freud was I wonder if that's not what I'm doing -- substituting altruistic pursuits for what's missing in my life? Well, is that so bad?

28

Involved, self-occupied, sometimes apathetic, tough, sometimes courageous, venturesome or defiantly ignorant, what's the point? Here on Earth, mischaracterization is largely the operant theme. Somehow, my lofty mischaracterizations allow fragmentation, malfeasance, and ill will to braid with innocence, surprise, wishes… and love. Love penetrates my countless dreams, sharing the aura of impulses and distractions, which is to say: my karma is my wish as now your karma is my wish. Why did I meet you now rather than long ago? In a time of a *when* that I should've?

It's been a whole month since I've gotten a letter from you. Didn't you get my last letter? Or, you're again far away? Hopefully not in some hospital in a foreign place with a broken leg? Or have you fallen in love? Or did you decide not to write to me anymore? I'm waiting for your telling me a secret.

Happy, happy Valentine's, with love

Fayewell

I spent a very blustery weekend escaping into the iris beds. The wind was warm and it was wonderful to sit in the grass, weeding and enjoying thinking of you. The lady who used to live in my house originally grew up on a tea plantation in Argentina. After years of moving around she eventually settled in Albuquerque. For thirteen years she spent all her free time planting apricots, roses, iris, and dozens of shrubs and trees. I feel whole here. Almost.

I would love to go back in time and see for myself how you played with people's eyelashes when you were a baby. One of my nieces loved eyelash kisses and asked for them whenever she could. After asking, she would close her eyes and peacefully wait. It was like a sacramental exchange. I imagine her now and tears come down my cheeks.

At the school where I've been working I'm enjoying the kids more than I ever dreamed I would. They're *all* lovable and affectionate. Most of them are bi-lingual and as far as they know I speak no Spanish. This is encouraged since they'll soon be in school and allowed only to speak English. So they've taking it upon themselves to "teach" me Spanish. *Esto es el papel; esto es la mesa.* They're so proud when I repeat it correctly. They have names like Javier, Arturo, and Isabella. We draw houses and trees on the blackboard, then play volleyball with balloons. They tell me it-was-a-dark-and-scary-night stories in broken English until they come to a word so scary it can only be said in Spanish. Their sweetness has not yet been trampled on or pushed away. Right now they live in a world of many surprises and few disappointments.

Do tell me about your trip to Colmar. I have a reproduction of Grünewald's Isenheim Altarpiece by my bedside. It's one of my favorite paintings, heartrending and joyous at the same time. The only thing I ever miss now is hearing from you. Once upon a time life was exciting then not. But all that was before I set out to find the path to the Infinite. And now, I've come to realize, that that's somehow through you.

Love, your Faye

I hope you'll get this on the equinox. Enclosed is my best cat whisker to mark the occasion. Note how sharp the face end of the whisker is. Just like a needle, I can weave it through the flannel of my nightgown. I have quite a collection now; easily enough to build three new cats if I had the other parts.

Love,
Faye

P.S. Curiosity is killing me. Please tell me the secret we were meant to trade. I've had to wait so long already.

Dear One

This morning was sunny and calm until I picked up my pen and paper. Just at that moment the wind began to howl. How fitting, as if the elements agreed with my decision to disclose all this overstepping of boundaries.

It was not unintentional and you did not misread the circumstances. I was so very happy to learn that you would be willing to have me visit. Perhaps I didn't outright say it in actual words that I would love to be with you, but it was there all the same. I have spent many hours dreaming of what it would be like. But, when I realized that you were getting my gist I got scared, awfully scared, and to protect us both I said that it wasn't so.

I don't know why I have come to love you, or how it happened that you touch me where I've never been touched before, even though we've never physically touched. I tell myself don't think "why?" It's enough that we hold each other someplace divine.

And, I do love you.

Fuinevere

The friend you mentioned in your last letter reminds me of someone I used to know. After his car accident he was not the same as before. He loved to be around people though he hardly spoke. At the oddest times, he would come up from behind and touch my hair, letting his hand slide down over and over again. It frightened me the first time. It was strange to see this big, strong man who was also as sweet as a child, be completely happy and content just to touch. And it wasn't just me; he'd do this to everyone he liked.

I wouldn't have thought you'd be having Spring in New York yet. We had twelve inches of snow here on Thursday. But now everything has resumed sprouting and the apple blossoms out my window are covered with buzzing bees.

I got some pussy willows for Easter. They are among my favorite springtime things. They are one of the first things I learned to say as a baby. "Pully whistles" I'm told is what I first called them.

What am I doing letting you know how close I feel to you?

Faye (or is it Isolde?)

I do love the words that are missing in the ending of your letter. Like a space become a riddle. I wasn't surprised. I think I already knew. I keep wishing I could ask. And get an answer.

At night I lie awake, wondering. I have all your letters. I keep them close to me because they are all I have of you. If my husband found them, his knowing about them would change everything, but not from some new understanding. I'd hate for him to think you are the reason for my leaving. But you would be the reason. I've stayed too long for it to not hurt him. Yet by staying longer I hurt him even more.

Notwithstanding my honoring the commitment I made, by writing to you I set something else in motion. I'm not willing to give you up. It feels a though I'm afraid of a million things and many of those things are good. I fear things that are good. It doesn't make sense. Do you wonder how we have become what we are to each other? I think it was David Hume who said, "The heart of man is made to reconcile contradictions."

I'm feeling the pain of too much tenderness. Wounded by my own understanding of love? Then bleeding willingly, joyfully. Because of you.

( )

Sometimes at night I watch the Moon and think that if you were looking at it too just then it would almost be like us being together. Everything I see, everything I care for, makes me think of you. Everything. I wonder how it's possible to miss what I've never had. You, your smile, your tenderness. Before we met I decided you didn't exist, so I wasn't looking for you. Now I ache from knowing you do exist yet are so far away. I dream of the string that guides me out of this labyrinth, back to you.

Thank you for the "imponderables" for my birthday. What is the aroma of stars lifting water? It takes my breath away.

I am your rosebud with swelling, diaphanous veil.

(Ariadne)

P.S. *He looked at her and inhaled her, she looked at him and inhaled him.*

–W. Somerset Maugham

I imagine how you must feel discovering the bees that have died when you open their hives in Spring. I so love that you have bees. That you make honey (or they do), and that you talk to them. I've been thinking about death, how quickly a life can be over. Yesterday I saw a highway wreck. I was so distraught my car scraped the divider out of shock.

This letter has been kissed just for you. I've kissed the letters I've received from you many times. And hold them close to me. Always inside me, you impart the wordless Vedas into my heart. Sometimes I don't know how I can endure life another minute away from you.

Love always.

P.S. The bees. What happens with them when they swarm?

Dreaming of wearing your favorite lipstick, dressing in my lace undies and heels, luxuriating beside you... Why do I love to dress up just to be by myself? I feel something below the threshold of ordinary awareness, with an array of magical clues regarding Persephone, Isis, Magdalene, karma, me. Metaphors help invent me, invent who I am... not the me that's defined by definitions. Me as a profound act of perceiving and giving love: a heart of rivers, a mind of silk, a womb of fire. I imagine you as a conjugal scientist, an agent of the evolving secrets, a karmic detective examining the misconduct of our existence. These are my metaphors for realizing my invention of you.

xxoo

My plan has been not to write until I'm a little more cheerful, but if I do that, I may not write for a long time.

I took a drive to El Rancho de los Colondrinas, a museum that includes a planting field with native crops, a *penitente mosada* (a church-like meeting place), two mills, a hacienda and the most wonderful public school house in New Mexico. Standing there, alone, I think, "a halo of mourning surrounds every desire achieved," allowing me to make some tentative peace with how it is that you and I are not together.

I try very hard not to let my emotions determine my overall disposition. I try to remember that what I feel is not necessarily reality. Someday, quietly sitting, doing the doing-nothing thing, perhaps it'll all dawn on me. Until then, I'm acutely aware of the time it takes to travel from one mood to the next.

With you always,

Faye (Beatrice)

P.S. I found a little prayer for you, by Franz Kafka. For your travels…

> You don't need to leave your room.
> Remain sitting at your table and listen.
> Don't even listen. Simply wait.
> Don't even wait.
> Be quite still and solitary.
> The world will freely offer itself to you,
> to be unmasked. It has no choice.
> It will roll in ecstasy at your feet.

Dearest One,

    I'm brimming with the need to tell you about the clouds over Abiqui Lake and what feels like. It feels like spinning on air...

Love and love again.

Fa-Eve

P.S. I miss your letters. Is it the Postal Service again? Or something else? It is too frightening to think that you haven't written because you can't. Or that you no longer want to.

6 Aug

My first reaction to your delayed writing was to wonder why you couldn't let me know, even briefly, how you felt. Didn't you think I'd worry about you by not hearing from you? How could you think that my responding to you might be a joyless task? Would that not invalidate what we've become to one another? Is it only me who is all nourished by this?

After your last letter I was trying to block out feelings and not ache for you in every corner of my life. Please, I want to say, just love me and be patient, but soon it'll be a year we've known each other and I'm still in the place where I was when we began. I haven't moved toward anything more real or happy. You have every reason to feel as you do. I sincerely do not know how to open the door and step forward. I envision an emptiness that paralyzes me. I don't understand what keeps me from moving toward you but the looming abyss of me upholding a ridiculous vow. I don't think you know what it's like to be so afraid that the only direction is to retreat further inside of yourself. Far away, in.

This must be tiresome for you, this waiting. If our places were reversed I might have already given you up as hopeless. But if you decide I'm worth bearing with a little longer then I believe it will be impossible for you not to see that you are the biggest part of everything real and true existing for me. In time, I know the emptiness will turn into possibility.

Missing you in a way that there are no words to describe,

Faya

I'm so glad I heard your voice. It's still with me. But I forgot so many things I had planned to ask if we ever did actually speak again. About your incessant travels. What your work is like. Your year in the seminary. The time when you milked goats. Your research endeavors. Your darker side.

I have more questions than ever. Or fewer questions? The words of your postponed letter jolted me out of thinking that I could go on forever waiting for a revelation. There is a new feeling of exhilaration I have about the unknown, about the future, about what needs to happen.

I so very much want to be with you. But what if I'm not what you want? That sordid refrain describes my horror. I couldn't bear any more broken dreams. Or, I can or should, and this is a test. And that's why I'm telling you this. I feel foolish blabbering about our destiny. I am not always in control of what I think, and sometimes it has results that don't agree with reality.

With my heart,

F

P.S. I so wish I could read the Akasha, the sacred script written in the sky. And once I did, I'd save Schrödinger's cat from that miserable quantum thought experiment. That's when I'll know how to go about accomplishing what I really want.

Ever since I read about you walking through your nearby cemetery I felt that you could feel me beside you. I want so much for you to feel me here, right now; it's one of those desert nights when the air barely moves, feeling like velvet on skin. The sky is clear, moonless, filled with stars. Perfect and as lovely as tears running down my heart.

Would all this be easier if I could look into your eyes? So to be sure that you knew how deeply I really feel? How could such closeness be endured?

Love,

Faye-Iseuld

P.S.
under the stars, stunned, soft, like skin, liquid in a puddle?
when the Earth is singed by the soles of my feet?
when dust swirls around cactus spines?and ivy?
love me in the deep? in the dark? when it pains to look at me?
when I'm the Rio Grande misting through reveries?
my shape shifting lips? my spine like the goddess Nût?
onto the surface of your life?
I'm your disaster breeding fruit…
offering enormity
singe and resurrection

I thought the phone would be a better way to communicate. It's not. Your first actual call to me now makes me lonelier. After your voice drifted away, I was left suspended in a nothingness that was numbing. Would facing you be better, or worse? I feel as though I live in limbo, sick to know I've got to abandon this pathetic arrangement I'm in, and sicker trying to figure out how.

I'm thinking of going to my family's farm in the Ozarks. Maybe they won't need any explanations, understanding that I just need to be at peace. Where I can paint and feel calm till I can be with you. Right now this emptiness is just torture. I'm sorry for the craziness. Forgive me. Sometimes I wish there to be other magic in the world besides you. There's not.

Meanwhile, with all the love I have,

Your-Idice

P.S. Are we dreaming to excess? For Novalis it was all about wetting the arts by Imagination. What is the depth of human feeling? Can words reveal it?

My feeling of "relief" regarding the latest in your life, your new lady friend, faded rather quickly after we hung up. Your second phone call, and now good-bye. So I did what any rational person would: had a drink and tried to sleep, then couldn't and started the whole process all over again. And again. I have absolutely no reason to be jealous. We only briefly met once. It was a year and a half ago and we've never seen each other since. A few letters and one other phone call.

I should never have wanted to know about this latest news. It's horrid. I feel like I've lost my senses. Worse, like I just lost my only lover.

My! I feel viperous; it's all about my own procrastination. I could've been with you, and I should be. I should feel happy for you that someone is in your life, caring for you. Instead I'm fuming. Right now I feel as though I don't have to be fair-minded or rational. I'm angry with you and me and everything.

Maybe you'll be happier without me ever being a meaningful part of your life. But I don't see how you could be. As new as your new love is, you might just miss me.

With (   ) ... and other things...

P.S. For years, I've reread the tale of Dwyn. She was a fifth-century Welsh maiden who fell passionately in love with a young man, Maelon. In time, with emotions running wild and chaotic, they fell into a great spat. Dwyn prayed to heaven asking why she had succumbed to this malady called love. An apparition appeared, giving her a potion to drink. Afterwards, the hapless Maelon was turned into stone. Dwyn immediately realized that a new and much larger malady now overwhelmed her.

I wasn't prepared for this sadness. My heart is dark and heavy, squashing me, accusing me of betraying it. Everything I see, hear, and do seems totally indifferent now.

I'm not sure if you're part of a vanishing tribe, or one to come. I do know that I've felt like sending your mother flowers for your birthday all this week. Though I've never met her, it's as if only she might understand how painful this is for me.

Eurydice

P.S. The more I caress your letters the more I can't bear to be without you, the more I can't resist you. Wasn't that the way with Eurydice who was unable to resist Orpheus' and his lyre?

I cant' say enough how sorry I am having taken so long sorting out my indecisions, my divorce. So much pain and garbage I've brought into your life. I wish I could've done it another way. I needed to be free, to be wholly for you. Please understand. I'm sorry more than you could know.

Please remember that sometimes things are not what they seem. I simply couldn't come to you back then. I just could not leave. I wanted to. Needed to. We needed to. But I couldn't. Don't judge me too bitterly.

Forever.

Q B S P

I dream awake, and my passion awaits expansion, toning, weighing, sifting, stirring, applying, giving birth to the touchable, intangible you. The wake of longing engages, time, discovery, reason. But, can *feeling* be asked to solve anything? The necessity for personalizing mystery—it's what I've always known to be a practice, a discipline—is a way of affirming my place *here*. The risk of this becoming the deepest of all wreckages activates the possibilities for me to regard the triune soul. And its splendor. No matter what...

Back in February you decided it would be best if we didn't write anymore. I thought at the time you were right. But for a different reason. Perhaps without you I'd grow stronger, make decisions I needed to make, do it on my own.

I thought I could do something wonderful for you, like leave you be and let you pursue your new sweetheart. But with all the time that's passed between us, I thought that you might have wondered how I was. I wonder that about you. And about the bees.

The last thing I want to do is darken your life again. You think there's no way to go back after all that's happened. You're wrong.

My heart pounded when the mailbox revealed your card. It has been so very long. I'll be spending Christmas alone now that I've finally left. I toyed with finding out if I still know how to go out on a date with someone, though I really don't wish to. Maybe just to make you jealous. Anyway, here's a rendering of my dating profile:

A quiet paradox of tender and bratty, a lover of aesthetics and outgoing solitude who enjoys secrets and surprises. A brazen nihilist whose optimism reveals itself through her choice of lingerie. A sometime glam-a-holic navigating the edges of darkness, shape-shifting by aiming to understand the secret within attraction; willing to wander into the order in chaos with lots of flirting…

Have a wonderful Christmas. I mean it, even if it means you'll be with your lady. Or should I call her girlfriend? Paramour? Lover? I'm sure she wants to know all about you since I'm sure she's fallen in love with you. But you're so protective of your privacy. What does anyone know about you? After all, what do I know about you, really? Enough of that, it'll be Christmas soon.

Be happy…

It snowed here last night. Beautiful. And this morning is so beautiful and so lonely all at once. I picked this flower for you in a protected spot near a sunny meadow in Pecos. I pressed it between these handmade paper sheets, and kissed you.

Q B S P

It's been a year and I've kept my word. Or your word. I'm not the one that said you'd never hear from me again. "Never" was your word, your wish. At least I've not phoned. Commendable, in some small way?

Such a long time, through the summer and its solstice, the third anniversary of our first brief and only meeting. It all passes silently as I feel I've lost the best part of me—you. Whenever I feel you in my memory I say a prayer.

Remember the beginning? How close we felt toward one another. I'm so sad for the way it all dropped like an injured fawn. I was so confused, being married then procrastinated my leaving. I dallied even telling you that I left. I felt completely directionless after hearing about your newfound love.

I hope you are truly happy. I know you can't let me know—your better judgment precludes it—but I'm wishing it…

…with all my heart

I'm thinking about the incontinent gods, those with cosmic dementia, with their limited future, their sensibleness worn-out. Do they continue hidden in somewhere in our psyches' depths? Do they surface from under the skin of seduction? Are they in the end spirit tricksters with an eye to having a helluva laugh?

Saturday morning and I'm still in my nightgown, wishing it were warm enough to be outside. These walls make me feel like I can't breathe. But somehow, I am breathing. And it's not the walls that are the problem at all.

I'm wondering where you are now, what city, what country? I only can guess from the faint postmark on that little card I received at Christmas? Do you have a shred of memory left of me?

 Thinking of you makes my body feel so real and suddenly you *are* real. It's very intense. I don't want to want you in this way. But so what about what I want. I don't have any control over it. My ideas of self-control or helplessness have been over-rated. Sex, you once wrote me, was a hieroglyph for spiritual love. I looked up the ancient Egyptian hieroglyph for love. It shows a man with his hand to his mouth, sometimes the hand is in his mouth.

I will tell you now, after all this time, that nearly every morning for all these years, alone, I touch myself, and cum over and over again while thinking of you.

P.S.
> while rubbing myself to ecstasy
> I become your pink instrument of gaze
> and flame and swamp and lava
> my fingers are your eyes, your revelation
> like the dawn antelope
> you are my divinity
> I am your becoming
> reaching

I should be looking for a way to make my heart still, find some kind of peace. Instead, I'm trying something new instead: making myself feel as bad as I possibly. How stupid. How incredibly ignorant I am for thinking *anything*.

I'm going to die from this. I'm sure of it. I know it. I know better than to let myself love you this much. I have always known it. It's terrifying. Prayers don't help me. Talking to God, or the universe, or the spiritual world doesn't relieve me.

For one split-second, one wild flash I felt it was okay, that no matter what happens it was worth it. That some things are worth wanting no matter what the cost.

P.S.   In-love displacing normalcy: why does it feel like falling? Untouched by remedies or advice, medicine or psychology, *why* does it feel like falling?

You told me nothing in your letter that gives me hope, but I read more in letters than just words. You seem so sure of yourself, so confident; very unnerving. But in secret I believe you are not stronger than I am, not stronger in your deepest heart. When I reread your letters now, I'm left in a room of sadness. Are you just masking what you really feel? I find myself wanting to know this difference in quality. Or am I in a dream? Maybe someday I will be able to ask you. The someday that will never be?

It seems that you have never been willing to ever tell me anything really clearly and straightforward. My experience is that reality has never been that way with you. Who can understand your idea of love? It's too complex. A simple conversation with you can be challenging. Now I'm the one who's angry. Here are all your previous letters. I'm returning them to your hands. With all the memories instilled in them. Forget about being friends. You win.

How did you do it? For years and all that water under the bridge, still, I can't relegate you to the back of my mind. From the day we met you've been here in my thoughts. Every single day. Sometimes my second self thinks I've conquered it. But just then some little thing touches the original me and I'm flooded. Your breath rolls over me and I can barely breathe. I sink into a pool of emptiness yet joined to everything.

Why are you so certain that I had "known" the outcome all along? That I wouldn't nor couldn't really see being with you? Not so. Even now, knowing it is the deepest haunting since I can't give up the dream of you. Probably never. To let go would be to lose myself, my identity. And yet, somehow, my life goes on.

P.S. I remember when you wrote long ago, mentioning the Holy Trinity. And now after all this time, I *am* relieved. How did Augustine put it? *Nulla est hominis causa philosophandi nisi ut beatus sit.*

I can't believe I'm letting this happen to me again. You were in my dreams all night. I woke up and said, "Okay, not real, go back to sleep, forget it." Then another dream of you, in a different place. I awoke again. We touched ever so softly with our hands. It was lovelier than any touch before. Ever in my life. Your dream elixir, does it work despite you?

It's wonderful and terrible to think of you. The thought catches me off guard, always. I was just getting used to *not* feeling again. Now with your words in front of me, my life is again turned inside out. Each time it reels me into what might have been. Will this ever go away?

You *never* did tell me your birthday. Or where you where you were born. You are the most secretive person I know, yet I know you have nothing to hide. It doesn't matter. I like to think that we came to Earth with the promise to someday be together. "Before," as my darling niece tells me, "when I was in Heaven and God was creating me," she says as a memory, not a fairytale.

Oh, God, this is where in closing "love" is often mentioned. I dare not.

Wishing as a subtle body, and a body that reaches... and why, in urging us, does this bring to life the awareness magnifying ache and affection. Warm and devotional. That's how I found myself threading my attraction into you. Threading onto all that never was across the panorama of loving. Attraction is a spirit-catcher yearning; its geography, abyss, and metabolism like a kingdom of all that ever was. Besides, an undying feeling between us shares absurdity, humor, heartache, and sense of supreme worth... ritualizing our imagination. Ritualizing lost time. Sacrificing ourselves, recovering one another.

Sweetheart
I miss you,
&
your
letters

yours,
(B)
Fatefully

Thank you for the card, as brief as it was. I knew that you were not so cold-hearted as to deny me that. You seem to know so much about so many of life's things I wonder if you will ever understand how it's possible to love beyond all belief and rationality. And then choose to remain true to your vows. To have your heart, soul and sanity hanging by a thread, day after day wondering if you're really that strong or just incredibly stupid. Of course, I hope you never need to know.

I'm still teaching. And painting. I love the kids, but the school system gets more absurd with each passing year. This thing called "education" happens in places where the walls are sterile, the curriculum dead, and the deeper things about life are disregarded. Hidden away. What's deeply true and real has to be discovered someplace else. Usually, that happens in the wrong places. Regrettably.

This might make you smile: I just read Van Gogh's letters to his brother Theo, and suddenly the brush strokes made completely new sense. Amazing the way his colors light the eye, and even more the way his words light the mind. Something that before was beautiful now becomes life itself. Should seeing art be influenced by discovering something about who made it?

May all your dreams come true,

Layla of the desert

P.S. I often imagine you in one of Van Gogh's paintings. My tongue instinctively wets my mouth. Then suddenly, through my lips, an emanation begins to lick the sky as I become mist-like, trembling.

Sitting here, alone but for my shadow, I'm searching to find the deeper reasons that contributed to what my mind (not my heart) calls a failure of love. I'm asking: How could've a palpable and immediate attraction connect me so intensely to you? Why does being in love seem to amplify of my soul so much? How is it that I could feel so out of my mind being in love with you? To where was my soul pulled by longing's intensity? Why did being in love with you make me feel so removed from the everyday world, overruling most o other pursuits, relegating other interests to interferences? Why did everything feel so uncertain being apart from you?

I know that you've been wounded by my love. I know that apologies can never simply fix what happened? Tell me: Do you believe there was a higher purpose for us to undergo this crazy blessed romance?

P.S. The spiritual kind of intimacy we shared was truly mythic. Then, when your patience could take no more, did the mythic disappear? Was it just a pretty face that made you drop the mythic, and me? Is she more special than I could ever be? I ask myself, ultimately, what would being without desire feel like? Anyway, while the beautiful places here are undoubtedly still beautiful, all enchantment for me has gone away without you.

Tonight I feel as though I could just press my hands firmly in your direction and transfer my love. Maybe I can.

I love what you wrote to me. Please, get well. Please. Promise if you need me you will let me come, no matter what? You need to be here on this planet. You're my bond to heaven. And earth.

with heart and soul

Beatrice (or who?)

P.S. I did check several times. No word yet on Atalanta Fugiens by Michael Maier.

Sweetie

On this eleventh of August, remembering the first time I laid eyes on you…
and all those moments in-between. I love you, mythically.

(B)

P.S. Mentioning moments, in-betweens, first times, and looking into the
larger arc of cosmic time and where we fit into the picture:

A *yuga* cycle is called *maha* (great) or *divya* (divine) *yuga*. One thousand such cycles forms one day of
Brahma, who governs the universe. One day of Brahma is 4.32 million x 1000 = 4.32 billion human
years. Each such day of Brahma is called a *kalpa*. His night also constitutes 4.32 billion human years.
During his day, life exists. In nighttime, no life exists. One complete day and night has 8.64 billion
human years.The age of Brahma is 100 years. Each year of Brahma has 360 days and the equal number
of nights. Thus, the total age of Brahma is 360 x 100 x 8.64 billion = 311,040 billion human years. i.e.
311.04 trillion years. This period is called *maha kalpa*.

The life span of the universe is one *maha kalpa*, i.e. 311.04 trillion human years. This time span is also
the duration of one breath of Vishnu (the supreme divinity in Hinduism). When Vishnu exhales,
thousands of universes emerge and one Brahma is born in each universe. When Vishnu inhales, all
universes are sucked in and Brahma dies. This cycle is non-ending and eternal. Thus, Vishnu is
considered eternal in Vedic terms. Considering the age of our universe, the period of *Satya Yuga* is 0.4x,
Treta Yuga is 0.3x, *Dwapara Yuga* is 0.2x and *Kali Yuga* is 0.1x where x is the time-span of one *maha-yuga*
cycle. Here, 'x' denotes 1 *maha-yuga* cycle.

In 1 day of Brahma, there are 14 *manvantara*. Each *manvantara* is divided into 71 *maha-yuga* cycles. The
total is 14*71 = 994x (*mahayuga* cycles). The remaining cycles (1 day of Brahma contains 1000 *maha-yuga*
cycles) are used to fill the gaps between *manvantara*. Before and after each *manvantara* (called *sandhya* and
sandhyamsa respectively), there is a junction of 1.728 million (age of *Satya Yuga*, or 0.4x) human years.
The total number of junctions are 15 (since there are 14 *manvantaras*). So the total gap period is = 0.4 *
15 = 6x. Hence the total is 1000 cycles, or 1 brahma day.

According to the Vedic texts, the current age of Brahma is 50 Brahma years plus 1 brahma day (we are
in the 1st day of 2nd half of brahma) and we are in the seventh *manvantara*, in the 28th turnover of its 71
cycles. The cycle, we are presently in is the *Kali Yuga*. The timeframe of the *Kali Yuga* is not known
exactly but it's about 8000 human years.

The current age of our universe (in terms of *maha-yuga* cycles) = (50 * 720 * 1000) -- 50 years * (360 days
+ 360 nights) * total no. of cycles in one day/night + (6 * 71) -- 6 *manvantara* each of 71 *maha-yuga* cycle
+ (7 * 0.4) -- 7 junctions or gaps for 6 *manvantara* + (27 * 1) -- we are in 28th cycle of 71 +
(0.4+0.3+0.2) -- In this cycle, we are in *Kali Yuga*. *Satya Yuga*, *Treat Yuga* and *Dwapara yuga* are 0.4x, 0.3x
and 0.2x respectively.

The total age of our current universe = (36,000,000 + 456.7) x = 36,000,456.7 * 4.32 million =
155,521,972.944 trillion human years.   :-)

Dearest

Only a little over 36 hours away from you and I can barely endure the thought of waiting any longer. This is more than surreal. Maybe because of getting only three hours sleep. It's so very strange trying to fall asleep without you even though I've never held you. And then the morning comes and it's nearly unbearable when I realize your not there. During the day I can hear your voice resounding inside me. Like all your letters became your voice.. It's hopeless.

I'm hopeless… and missing you mythically!

QBSP

It's late and I'm very, very tired. Marla is sleeping with me in bed tonight so I don't feel so alone. Maybe we'll just say prayers, cat-prayers. Will I ever stop wondering about you a thousand times a day?

I'm trying to keep all my thoughts at bay tonight. Only cat-thoughts and thoughts of you and my mind on a pillow.

good night...

P.S. It's after midnight. Did I imagine you renamed me Cherry Bottom?

Marla got a major emotional cat disturbance today. She gets these sometimes. I think she takes after me.

Confession. Of a special variety. I've gone into sugar overload. Not intended but your sweet gift to me just was wonderful and I want you, so badly. I ate them all, during the day. Forgive me but it's the closest I came to touching you.

Does trying to understand romance make things less romantic? Romance makes life special in a way it has never been before and will never be again. With all the trying, should we be calling the whole venture exercises *for* romantic understanding? Why did I ever feel that romance could remedy the head, the heart, or both? It hasn't for me. Just the opposite. Does acting yearning out, like giving sweets and treats, improve the chances of "figuring things out"?

I just missed the mailman to send you a cat whisker. I'm off to the post office soon.

Soon…

Darling

Separation is the worst feeling ever. I think Emily Dickinson once wrote, "Where thou art, that is home."

You're the one I thought I'd never find. You are so precious. This is like a lovely miracle and yet a nervous miracle. I'm with you always and you with me a thousand times a day. And at night, and in-between.

I love you to death

Sweetheart

I haven't a clue why it's so difficult to just board a plane and meet. Three times already - your emergency and then mine and then this. It's been crazy. Why? I dream of a life together and it's a real dream though I'm tired of feeling nightmarish when our plans are once again interrupted.

Thank you for what you sent on romantic understanding.

I'm so glad you were away overseas when I sent those letters back, innocently saved by your landlady. Bless her. And now I've gotten them back, as if repetition were itself magical, shaping destiny. Isn't the future the strangest thing?

Mein Hertz ist Dein

Hi Baby

It was so lovely finally hearing your voice again even if it was on the other side of the Atlantic. I feel more distressed than ever. I'm not sure why. If we ever could be together I will never take it for granted. Promise.

It must be awful being stuck so far away. I've almost completely abandoned the hope of having steady nerves again in this lifetime. Marla is spending eighty percent of her time under the bed since I've been worried about you.

Miss you awfully

Faye

To my dearest one, the rarest rabbit of them all -

possessor of my heart

my dreams

Better than Belgian chocolate truffles is a letter from you! I so need your strength and confidence. Our lives will be better together. Sacred and beautiful and blessed.

Sweetie, please come and get me as soon as you can. And for all our days. Yes, yes, yes!

I will be for you all I dream of being.

Mythic 2

P.S. from *The Ring of the Dove* by Ibn-Hazm (c. 1022 AD)

To make a signal with the corner of the eye is to forbid the lover something; to droop the eye is an indication of consent; to prolong the gaze is a sign of suffering and distress; to break off the gaze is a mark of relief; to make signs of closing the eyes is an indicated threat. To turn the pupil of the eye in a certain direction, and then to turn it back swiftly, calls attention to the presence of a person so indicated. A clandestine signal with the corner of both eyes is a question; to turn the pupil rapidly from the middle of the eye to the interior angle is a demonstration of refusal; to flutter the pupils of both eyes this way and that is a general prohibition. The rest of these signals can only be understood by actually seeing them demonstrated.

All this while my heart knows that to be apart from you is darkness and want; I've known this from its very beginning. Until there was you there was just absence. Now, divine ache. If I close my eyes I can feel your arms around me, your lips touching mine. And the world stops.

What we have is breathed by heaven, truly. I feel some kind of dark power has kept us apart. We will overcome it.

"In the mind there are no answers; in the heart there are no questions."

QBSP

Part 2

The *vena amoris*, the vein of love,
is said to travel with risk on a wager, on a gamble.

Midweek, I drove to the old Shaker village in Hancock on a visit to what could be called "Simplicity." As you perhaps know, the Shakers were noted for their disdain of worldly frivolity, their love of craft, work and cooking. And their untiring limbic devotion to God. Oh, and their commitment to celibacy, a basic premise for their decline. Look anywhere and you'd catch a glimpse of "force evolving to form" (or form to force depending on the perspective). Enclosed are a few photos I took of their gardens, the community's main building, and the round stone barn, beautifully centric, ingenious. I wish I could send you the aromas of their lemon balm and the smoothness of their wooden tables. I can't help being of the mind that there was a real excitement in everything they touched while not touching each other.

Sometimes it feels freer to speak to a stranger. There's little need to apologize. Let's just say we're no longer strangers. I'll plant that thought here where but a few Shakers are left waiting to meet their creator. And about that other thing: What, for some is *belief* lived in Goethe as *fact*; he once remarked that wherever he found necessity, there he saw God.

All best,
Tristan

On the heels of driving winds, a cold front from the north dropped six inches heavy snow in as many hours. Not to be outdone, the sky grew another ice storm resulting in a cacophonous outburst leaving fallen limbs everywhere. A month early for the season. Several of my beehives were lost to a huge birch that fell on top of them. The next day everything was clear sunny October orange again. I started up the chain saw and began undoing the enormous mess.

After those meteorological consequences, in devotion to the girls at large— those of the bee yard, that is—I began to gather up the hive's stragglers without yet finding their queen. A few dozen of those perturbed decided I was probably an uninvited animal and began stinging me with all their fury. I had to take flight. So much for heroism. I did suit up later… and found her majesty!

You mentioned you still believe in fairy tales. Their magic, yes? That they're sort of like a "chance" meeting on a jet moving toward a two thousand mile conversation?

Tristan

Distance is playing wild with us all, sculpting perceptions like silly-putty as we get answers to potentially live by. Mostly though, answers explain nothing. Sometimes we have to let go of knowing so that feeling becomes our data, conviction our proof.

Tristan

P.S. After all was settled with the hives and the fallen trees, I hiked half way up the nearby mountain. Then slid down on a wedge of cardboard plowing into the wind, imagining holding you close.

We spoke briefly that time of going beyond the limits of ourselves. Moving into the expanse of someone else's heart. Expansion of an ethereal sort. Am I sounding like Mr. Wizard?

What I wish to say is that, somewhere in the back reaches of my mind, a voice utters the word "mythic" when I think of what we started. A story that awaits its characters' next move. Like a dream's starting place entering a chronicle of *something* being foretold.

Tristan

Can't quite say it, but it was…

… an image of a winged, blindfolded youth, bow held, arrow cocked. Drawing the string back he's merciless. Why such enchantment? Was it the melodiousness of your voice? Or a visit of an angel fastening into my ears?

Or is it my sense that, behind the words, I let the world disappear?

Tristan

P.S. From Goethe's Tale of the Green Snake:

"What is more noble than Gold?".
"Light" replies the Snake.
"And what is more refreshing than Light?" asks the King.
"Speech" replies the Snake.

I as well often wonder to what life aspires. I think of those Gothic cathedrals, many of them I visited years ago, with their mounting crowns piercing skywards. Spires reaching for the firmament. Their uppermost tip meeting heaven, touching the divine far above worldly noise and its shadows. As if all material things were a loneliness needing to find company and solace in celestial imagination.

Spires. Were they sprung from some inspirational need to touch? Touching the invisible? Being a youngster, I used to ask, as most children do, what will I one day become? Now, in increasingly large doses, I aspire toward being still, waiting. Waiting to touch the divine. Then again, if I may be as inconsistent as you say *you* are: to be more like lightning in a flash, to dissipate into pure possibility.

Or maybe I'm just dreaming of kissing you.

Tristan

P.S. "There is but one Temple in the World and that is the Body of Man. Nothing is holier than this form. Bending before men is a reverence done to the Revelation in the Flesh. We touch Heaven As we lay our hand on another's body" — Novalis

Contemplating softness, silence, syllabaries, and unthought thoughts. Embracing you while in the gesture of my longing. Filled with paradoxes and innocence, drunk into imaginings. Readying to steal and return your gods, and you mine; readying to remonstrate with each other's demons. Acts of closeness in this cleft of not-knowing.

With silence and unthoughts

Somewhat expectantly flew back to the U.S. after work plans changed.
Detoured to Delft, then Amsterdam. Got back to the States on Thanksgiving
day which was as well a special birthday, my Mom's. I arrived just before
dinnertime. Within the hour a celebratory mood carried on minus my brain
from lack of sleep and jet lag. It was all I could do to stare at the cake and
wonder why everyone was speaking English.

When I finally did get back to my place and piles of mail, there was your
letter and YES your picture with that smile! Did you smile like that when the
"magic thing" I sent you arrived? Say yes and your going to get more than
magic you can manage. Remember if anyone asks, tell them you've started a
necessary leaf collection, and stare them down.

Tristan

P.S. A silly limerick came to me while cruising over the Atlantic:

> the philosopher Hamann was no slouch on the lute
> his fingers the instrument did suit
> inspirationsl for the Sturm und Drang
> "Ja! *now* we're having fun"
> mused the Zeitgeist with a Teutonic toot

I don't feel like being a smartass today so I'm just going to welcome the St. Christopher medal from you. I genuinely appreciate that it comes from you. To quote Paracelsus, "The saints have a certain time during which they may exist." Me too, as unsaintly that I am.

I feel that writing to you is like extracting the fire of life from my heart and holding it up? To ineffable vision? To you? Just to say it reveals the splendor I feel thinking of your smile.

Tristan

P.S. Someday we'll talk about the Isenheim Altarpiece. It holds a light deeper than the understanding.

Why do fantasy and invention seem so necessary in our lovely communiqués? Perhaps they ripen destiny with a personalized yet universal longing. Even if indefinite in specific intentions, they in some way encourage and curate Imagination.

Do we need to be forgiven for having our attractions? Pardoned for our fantasies? Guilty for what or how much we wish? For our attempts to fulfill those wishes? Our questions to the gods ought include, "What do *you* do with our longing? Our satisfactions? Our disappointments?"

Trist I am

Dear Faye

Are you familiar with the Matachines Dance? I imagine you are. During
December, on snowy days or cold nights the matachines appear in Bernalillo,
Jemez Pueblo, Alcalde and probably dozens of other villages throughout
northern New Mexico. Peter Garland, the composer, told me it was one of
the crucial things that influenced his soul to settle in that geographic area.
The dances are a strange and hypnotic performance, part sword dance, part
morality ritual, and part ancestral magic. There's the contrasting of brilliant
colors and masks and costumes against the enormity of the immense desert.

Witnessing the dance, everyone gets drawn into their rhythm and spell.
Little girls are dressed in white, their inspired grandfathers become clowns.
Old rusted cars and dilapidated trailers are the sole connection to the ordinary
world.

Tristan

P.S. As a youngster I'd sometimes calculate how much or how long of
something, like, "It's been ____ seconds since the birth of Christ. It is now
____ seconds and counting…"

The solstice arrived with the first the carillon concert at Manhattan's Riverside Church. Those attending the hand bell concert in the great church below found ourselves clouted into a festival of sonic resonances. Eight distinct hand bell choirs, each sounding out their peels of brightness, overtone dissonances and jubilations. Then, gracefully, slowly, they emerged from their far corners, heading up the aisles. Congregating from the transept to the apse, together they chimed away into a lovely harmonic convergence.

What's crisp and punctuated can also be rounded and precise with a hand bell. What's overtone-chaotic in a huge carillon is pitch perfect with a hand bell. Now, put hundreds of bells together, *solisti musica*. They're sharp and perfect like a cat's whisker. Yet round, and warm too. I'll have to write to my old friend Mumbai Tiger, telling her about you. She has the largest whisker collection in the Northern Hemisphere. A cat lovers' envy. She'll smile when I mention your collection. "Sisters from way back" she'll likely say.

Tristan

P.S. I'm dreaming of a carillon with perfect noise, shaping sound into a music attenuating into a perfect wishker.

P.P.S. "When you hear the soft harmonies of the choir's singers, some taking high and others low parts, some singing in advance, some following in the rear, others with pauses and interludes, you would think yourself listening to sirens rather than men, and wonder at the powers of voices … whatever is most tuneful among birds, could not equal. Such is the facility of running up and down the scale; so wonderful the shortening or multiplying of notes… that the ears lost their power of judging…transporting the soul to the society of angels." — John of Salisbury, Bishop of Chartres

The arrival of the luminarias-to-be (by which you have now perennially established your complete and utter sweetness) ushered in a pure luminescence, an aura for always. Hurrah for me returning to this continent. The votive box filled with candles says, "for religious and home use." Hilarious distinctions.

That secret thing you wished to know: That as I very young child I loved to touch eyelashes. For hours I could do this, and would do so if allowed to. Still to this day I dream of that sensation, like the softest explosion throughout the body. When I think about what hands and fingers do, what they've learned, I thank all those eyelashes I touched as a kid. The memory clear as a bird, pleased as a cow, as single-minded as an attentive feline.

Luminarias!

Tristan

P.S. Under the suggestive power of Eros, I awakened from sleep touched by a wondrous new power. I've now admitted to myself that letters can be like kisses radiating a deep faith through the senses.

Freeing oneself of the head into the open heart is like a dreamer divested of a monkey on his back. With so many cautionary tales as reminders, me harboring a certain detachments isn't a new thing. Sometimes the feeling that resides between me and someone feels so vast that I pray to Nature as if she were my closest confidant beseeching me, impelling me into "the closeness."

Sometimes the gap ushers in beautiful rays illumining my imagination. Despite myself.

For now, I will take in you encouraging me to quit being so aloof. I know what I should be doing, revealing my heart. It may be a struggle for me. If it is will you tell me to go be detached somewhere else?

Tristan (or is it Dante?)

Dear Valentine,

    I envision a play of morning shadows in your room. Goosebumps all over, with your arms crossed over your shoulders, over your breasts. Streaks of light rebounding off your skin. A heartfelt glow glides across your face. I imagine that your thighs are butter-soft as they slowly rub together. Outside, the cicadas sing.

Tryst

(In my dream we're sitting in your iris beds, unfastening our shoes, tilting back our heads to better see the sky.) *Este es mi cuerpo, esta es mi alma.* Shall I draw you the sphere of heaven; trace our spirit in the dirt?

Will you draw them now for me?

Yes! (My hands are cupped, forming a ball).

Please, I can't wait....

I will, but I need some water....

But, where's the water....?

Let's use our saliva....

(We wet our palms, pressing the wetness into each other's faces.)

What is it to be baptized through the spirit of your beloved? *Este es mi cuerpo, esta es mi alma. Este es mi espíritu.*

Tristan

This morning I prepared a sweet nectar for the bees. Spring is a crucial time, it'll determine their fate for the rest of the season. They're just about out of honey with hardly any blossoms happening yet. The nectar I'm making consists of chamomile tea and sugared water. They love it!

About my so-called Catholic "vision": When the notion dawned in the underworld that love is conditional, the resident demons began to eat people's dreams. Since then, they piss in to the wide world of undigested longing, defecate into the inner life of desire. They strategize, generate disenchantment, stupidity, shadows, fantasies, and hope.

For me, Christ is the ultimate source of all genuineness. And the paradoxes of selfhood, selflessness, grace and tragedy, bestowing a deep sense for practicing existence on Earth in the way that's worthy of us human beings. So, about my drawn-out incarceration at Sacred Heart: surviving that ordeal provoked two strategies: dealing with the fearing the consequences of my deeds in the hereafter. And dealing with those nun creatures with their foreboding habits which was enough to shrink most thoughts of faith, hope and love. I'd ask: How did Infinite Goodness cook up the righteousness that in advance judges and commands to DO NOT? That's the faith I was born into. And that's what I dealt with until I couldn't.

Tristan

P.S. If you again write a letter to me as you did last time beginning with: "I love you so enormously…" Stop right there. STOP. Add a period. Sign it, kiss it, post it. Okay?

Despite the ever looming reality of months of cold, one morning everything changes. Forsythia buds sprout their yellows and fragile green. Purple, blue, and white crocuses spot the ground; softer-than-anything pussy willows advocate for more light. A week ago we had snow, now the bees are heavy with pollen heaped over their legs.

Discovering a waterfall high in the mountains, the old Shinto masters would pray to the resident god. That particular god and no other would be the personality of that waterfall. Prayers then were acts of reverence. Intimate acts of devotion to the spirit of falling water: devoutness becoming wholly present to the god. So much presence regarding what is, and what isn't.

One of my best friends visited here last week. A severe accident ten years ago damaged his brain so he has a type of amnesia. He can remember the qualities and personality traits of places and people, but no single incident, no memory or event in his or anyone else's life before the accident. We talk often. Every now and then he asks me what happened in the summer of…? Or did we ever…? We did many crazy things in our early days, some of which he doesn't believe and with good reason: I've pulled a few tricks on him to engage the spirit of his "former self": Like the time I told him "though you don't remember, we hang-glided down the Chrysler building back in the late '80s." Awestruck, he believed me for months. Now with any of my stories, he just laughs and laughs, looking closely at me to discern clues that could betray reliability.

Last night, I told him a bit about you and me, our meeting, our story and letters. He took it all in attentively, then nodded. Slowly, a smile breaks, then widening, he starts to laugh. Seeing him laugh, I break into a smile. Soon we're both bellowing since he's not sure whether to believe any of it or not. And I'm not sure I could convince him it's true.

Laughing, he says, "tell me about the time we climbed the Tetons half-naked, humming Mozart and looking for bears." "Okay," I reply.

Tristan, aka Willaby

Like desire drawn from the depth of feeling, navigating the indefinable, gradually becoming an art. When we seriously decelerate our impulsively propelled self-image, we experience an wish for tenderness, our souls pervaded with openness, warmth, vital contact. Without struggle, without need to constrict or rush the pleasure-giving moment, we safeguard the integrity of an ever-freshening intimacy.

Despite disappointments, dilemmas, jubilations and joy, I feel my devotion sculpting desire into an ocean of possibility. An ocean in which I discover desire producing limbs whose impulse is founded on the wellspring of inspiration. It's aim, as I experience it, is to form a conduit en route to love.

I dreamt of you in *my* iris bed right here in the front meadow. Violet raying irises, with you sitting in your nightie, scooping playing in the dirt. Looking upwards as the clouds bent down, the sky kissed your nose as the flowers all around shuddered.

When I awoke, your letter was in bed with me, I fell asleep while holding it. You're in my dreamtime a lot. Especially since my imagination is the only place I *can* see you. And anyway, physical eyes are limited by physical distance but dreaming eyes create imaginations. With those I envision your softness, smile, and lips.

When I my friend came by again last week (the one with the accident I wrote you about) I showed him the bundle of your letters. He looked, silent for a long time, like some oracle. An uncommon lucidity appeared over his face as he looked up and said: "You love her even with all her pain and indecision. She's probably married and lives clear across America. She's beautiful, she's in love with you and neither of you have any idea of what to do about it."

With love and undulations,

Will &Tristament

97

Knowledge is the goal of the self as self embraces its higher consciousness even with all the enigmas. To locate meaning, the self inhales its visions. Then exhales a world made of imaginal substance. The substance making the world tip on its axis.

Smooch,
Tr-Distain

P.S. I always wanted to write: "typical is a archetypally appalling word." Not sure why but I wanted to write it, and so I did.

Six or seven birthday wishes for my dearest:

- We're get to sleep under a huge blanket

- We feel hypnopompic stirrings

- You receive from me two eyelash kisses

- We can feel our pulses braiding together

- Our lips meet

- We make waffles for breakfast

- ...

Love,
always

Flew back to New York yesterday just for a two of days until off again. I got to explore the street life up near the Hispanic Museum. Surprise! Their El Greco's are superb. And they've got Goyas and some beautiful works by Zubaran. I know you'd love them all. The city is wonderful yet there's a sadness here that is different from the sadness in Seville, Madrid, Barcelona. It's the unrelenting boxiness and straight lines all around. I feel more contracted on this hardened island than in other cities.

After finding an affordable hotel room, I met an old friend Lothar at Café Taci for dinner. Near Columbia U. Luckily, it was opera night featuring Piccola Callas (the nickname he gave a petite opera singer who he likens to Maria Callas) sing an aria from Fernando Celia's L'arlesiana. Piccola Callas is a outstanding soprano. And he's in love with her.

I didn't get your letter in Switzerland, but they said that they'll forward it to London where I'll be next week. I still carry the after-image of our first meeting in my mind. It distracts me during the most inopportune moments. Like when a waiter asks if I'd like more coffee. I look at the cup and smile. Or at the museum, the guard had to tell me three times the museum was closing before I heard him. Is this some sorcery casting its net around me? Making sport of me? Capturing me? Readying to devour me?

Love,
XYT

P.S. I love how your voice blossoms my imagination…

P.P.S. "You just learn to cope with whatever you have to cope with. I spent my childhood in New York, riding on subways and buses. And you know what you learn if you're a New Yorker? The world doesn't owe you a damn thing."

— Lauren Bacall

Thank you for the fish-whistle you sent! I'm certain the fish can't resist it. I imagine that it warns them or entertains them, depending. And yes, I do need one 'cause it's a heart line, a New Mexico /New York heart-line on extra-glow.

I'm convinced what's between us isn't just fantasy or obsession. If you are a dream then you're *the* dream at the tip of my horizon, the vista of everything that *could be* and should be.

Good night, darling

Trisagion

P.S. You asked if I was ever married. Engaged long ago, the relationship met its perimeters and its fate. And mysteriously, accidently, I dropped a stunning diamond ring off a houseboat which confirmed that was the end of that.

You wanted to know about the bees. They are my own little sweeties, dancing girls on the hexagonal rays of heaven. Their six-sided honeycomb reminds me of quartz crystals directed skyward. In honeycomb, Nature expresses pure form, pure deliciousness. I'm sending you some of last autumn's honey. I call it Yellow Orbit Honey. Liquid love.

You get sweeter to me every day. I can feel inside your words, hear things unheard by me before. The pully-whistle feel of your words is lovely liked velvet morning. We've touched one another from inside out.

I remember when I was kid, Grandma would take me to afternoon novenas at Holy Trinity Church. I really would rather not have gone. She dragged me even under protest. But the sentiment would change when I saw her light a candle. Her eyes would close and she disappeared into the light, becoming more beautiful.

Orphical

P.S. You kissing your letters with lipstick for me is a significant visualization of devotion. I close my eyes and feel the light of your lips on the paper. Like tulips brimming red. Two lips, tulips, two lips…

Sweet One

I'm now looking at a heavy glass paperweight; an orb I received long ago. It's made from the ashes spewed from a volcano. Burgundy deep bursts and swirling helixes within. A dance of bubbles and elliptical traces Motions of centrifugal intensity with crystal clearness and clouds of dreaming. An image of my feelings for you.

I feel I'm tethered to one thought, that of you resting in my arms head on my heart. A feeling that emanates as if a blessing. Having stepped outside my lesser self, there's no question, just the simplicity of it being true.

When I inferred your trepidation about us having a phone call, I thought of us starting with a silent intro, one cryptic and confident. After that, a silent au revoir with a hint of kissing.

(For always
Pierced-
True (

P.S. In my dream last night I was wearing a dark suit, a yellowy shirt sporting a lavender-colored bowtie adorned with Egyptian hieroglyphs. You slowly came to me, hugged me, pressing your newly highlighted lips firmly onto my collar.

Curiosity evolves an aperture into attentions newly discovered, enacting a mythology through ritual and imagination. Ours. A mythological romance claiming the story of what holds together our love.

Darling,

Along with any surreptitious references, I brimmingly await you telling me
what your fingers do *down there*.

Overflowing with
lust & Smooches

Tryst-kindlein

In loosening the body, the active imagination becomes an exercise in joy-absorption. A commitment to aura spotting hidden colors. Desire spying on itself. A chemical amazement. All of that in order to see so as to become adept at feeling the center... of everything. I'm here looking out from within...

Such an erotic-episophical campaign à la reverie into this inter-dimensional portal. Like entering some secret order within chaos. Why is the verb *pleasuring* largely absent from general communication? As many gods freely do, shouldn't we? How pleasuring can enlighten the body exists via our fingers, our ears, lips, between legs and hypothalamic transmissions.

Back in the day I read Stendhal who believed the essence of love was fantasy. Then, reading Proust, that the essence of love had to do with losing the self through the subtleties of nostalgia. Perhaps desperation. I met those feelings as if they were characteristic of longing for death. Then the modern—does *modern* mean anything anymore?—version of that sentiment seems like a voyage into resignations. Worse than death. I feel I could go out of my mind with all the psycho madness brewing all around. But what would the lunatics call my divine mania?

By opening to love we open to heartbreak. Loving like this risks all. I don't wish for anything different. Only that we climb deeper into this wish, whose mystery we need to uncover; it's the truest depth of wishing where there's no long any residue of a wish.

Remember, I will love you even if it means bearing all the heartbreak in the world.

Tristan

Many years ago, the Times printed a letter I sent in. I'm not sure why I was so moved to write it. Aside from fly fishing and soccer, I'm not at all a fan of sports.

Then considering the dozens of people who've passed into the afterlife who've been close to me in deeper ways, my letter (which mysteriously reappeared, falling out of a book about the alchemist Michael Maier) has mostly to do that I get what you mean about truth, honesty and the horrors of letting them slip into different meanings.

Tristan

ONE OF BASEBALL'S GREATEST PLAYERS

To the Editors:

Aside from an occasional Mets game, I'm no follower of baseball. I have, however, watched Bartlett Giamatti's moves from the sidelines over the last few years and have been struck by the man's integrity and wholesome vision both as a public figure and educator. There was little surprise for many, I suppose, when he left Yale to become the National League President - after all, although he never cut into the Big League, wasn't baseball his first and enduring love? The passion for something is, to my mind, the explanatory factor here. Wasn't this a chance to play, not physically, of course, not simply vicariously, but in the internal marrow of the game - its spirit - guiding its balance and course?

It turned out to be quite a game though - tough - and playing this game wasn't for a score. No. And it was a game that could never be lost without consequences that gnaw at its foundations. I'm sure the Pete Rose affair was far from being merely unpleasant. It was in all likelihood agonizing for Giamatti - making this game brutally intense. With one of the great stars of baseball, a hero and legend for many, transgressing baseball's honor, this was saying something about the course of the game, that the meaning and integrity of gamesmanship are no longer self-evident; that baseball is no exception to the kind of unenlightened self-interest permeating our times.
But the game is an exception! Giamatti's decision produced no score, no popularity, nobody won, nobody walked away happy. But silently, the game stood victorious.
Although the crowds may not be mourning the passing of one of baseball's great players, one can only say Giamatti played a hell of a game and he played with heart for the spirit of the game.

(Name withheld on request)

Darling Fayette,

I sometimes wonder about the consequences of the our thoughts, our shedding feelings onto the world, our deeds and effect. All of it to a degree influences the soul of the world whether or not those influences establish obvious physical changes in our environment. How do all the indescribable and imponderable drives, notions, musings, feelings, emotionality, and unconscious and subconscious emanations from billions of people influence what's around us. Most of it happening with hardly much reflection on our part. It's dizzying.

At their core, our sensual and intellectual faculties comprise a twofold unity. "Two forces of one Power," as Coleridge understood it. There's built-in imagination regarding understanding as well as what's not-yet-understood. And likely, the never-to-be-understood. "Extremes meet" was another of Coleridge's maxims. Maybe not unlike Reason meeting Imagination, Imagination meeting Understanding, Understanding meeting Intuition, Intuition guiding Sensibility. Forgive me, the universe seems to be disappearing with all this babbling and me with it.

Your T

P.S. "Thenceforward the Sun, the Moon and the stars can go forward on their path in peace, for I know not whether it be day or night, and the whole universe disappears before me."   — Goethe, The Sorrows of Young Werther

So many creatures: snakes, spiders, ants, wasps, crocodiles, flowers, mushrooms, lichens. It all feels "unimpossible." And all of us in the world who seem to become more and more like vague presences, reaching into our own vanishing point. I'd like to think that vanishing can open to a refreshed horizon of possibilities. Bearing that in mind, I think compassion and tenderness are our everyday angels. How else can we withstand so many concerns and uncertainties?

Missing you, mythically

P.S. "You do not measure the fruit of your actions. You have to measure the obligation of your actions. You have to find out what's the right thing to do. That is your duty. Whether you win or lose is not the issue." —Vadana Shiva

The Unseen draws us beyond the mind's limits. Our heredity and histories, our countenance and masks portray several of *who* we are. Some we arrive with, bound by karma, fate, proclivities; others we put on, mold our personality for reasons of survival, requirements, fantasies, enjoyments. The draw of the Unseen takes our histories, masks, our karma, coalescing all them in a cauldron of longing, and often pain. We couldn't be blamed regarding much of it predetermined. So with the many obstacles to our togetherness: Can love exist between two people but function as if in separate universes, with separate plans?

It's true when you say this crazy romance, its precedents and variations done over and over. Countless times, time and again to no avail. Each failure, a grimacing of fate, each reminiscence a haunting of the heart. Assuming that we can solve the difficulties our circumstances have given us feels like inviting a specter into the scene. I think we both feel it, but the awful thing is that our solutions appear like the one another's agony.

Are you too feeling there's been more craziness than actual love in either of our lives?

> Not with a fools gold but with a hidden gold
> that I call love

Love offers a great mystery of the heart, its animation, worth. The greatest gift we can bestow on ourselves and the world is the making of our noblest character.

This is the prayer I now voice aloud to Holy Mary: Blessed be She who sows and weaves, who divines our desires and lights new paths. Amen.

Your right, I know less about long-term relationships than you do. Though perhaps I know a thing or two about how I feel. The consequences of your indecision has made you descend into self-pity. I'm trying to resist the rage brewing me.

I hate to think that we confused fantasy with love. Maybe that's what's happened. I've all along wished to think that desire is only quenched by a greater fire that helps accomplish what has to happen, manifesting what's true.

And about that inviolable sense of safety and solitude by being there for another: How could we be satisfied with anything less than being in each other's heart, soul, and body. Love and devotion to someone real.

I want to scream, and scream!

Will-be-done

P.S. What would this all look like if you weren't so afraid? How could I have done anything different to help you not be afraid?

Being angry about our situation is perhaps not so awful. I imagine anger can be love boiling over. And, sometimes love, aside from how crazy it has made us, is, deep down, a hallowed hurting.

I remember as a boy, my bedtime prayer bidding the Christ child to come support me to be pure and humble, inviting him into my heart with the words, *Mein Hertz ist Dein*— my heart is yours.

Love in all lengths of desire
and possibilities…
Mein Hertz ist Dein

My courageous self says I ought never wake out of this dream. Rather, climb higher into its holy madness. I sometimes hear your guardian angel speak with no misgivings once we created this shrine around us. With the pain of vacancy like a hawk bounding off the mesa, climbing in the sky.

If we could clarify this mess of ours would we be delivered into some enlightened approach that our dreams seek? Or be left with more unanswerable question? Ever wandering on our own, figuring it out?

Regardless, I can see your cheeks becoming red as they press against my unshaven face. Your hair tossed by my hands, my fingers feeling between your toes. The world scurrying under the shade of our clutching.
One day I will paint your lips deep red on the bank of the Rio Grande, in imitation of all things divine.

What is the meaning of flesh on flesh? What is the meaning of our circumscribing one another?

Odysseiot

Missing you has become sometimes my tomb, sometimes my shrine. When I'm not totally drunk with you, I take counsel with who I've become, a remedy in the guise of a disease. Love can be a bloody thing. My heart is full with you. In between each pulse, the silence is a taste of our higher dwelling. I realize good sense and being down-to-earth are useful strategies though neither are a footing for creating majesty. Yet we've become a fire, a fire consuming itself, creating majesty but not reality.

William Blake once remarked, "Eternity is in love with the production of time." Since there's no doubt that eternity is in love with you and me, so regarding all of what keeps us apart I've more than once inquired: Why is it taking so much time?

Able-hard

P.S. Strangeness arouses wonder when we do not understand; and imagination when we do.

— Cecco of Ascoli

Yet some much of you is a mystery. I planted coriander today by the huge rocky protrusions near the hives. I trust someday to put a fresh seed in your mouth. Watching the bees and how they're consumed with making sweetness out of nearly nothing, is a taste of the promise of love. Even if I seem to understand their world less and less, I taste the honey of you coursing inside of me. How else can I account for acknowledging what's been missing all the while in me?

always, always
Trrrr

Sweetheart

Given your incessant uncertainties of what you need to do to be with me, what will become of our togetherness if it loses moment? What will become of us if you can't manage to take a next step? This is withering us. And for reasons that even baffle you. What's indulgent about this kind of loop is that it makes everything feel as though you are lost deep in some abyss with no way out. If you're afraid of having regrets, those regrets will paralyzed everything. Alone in your desert, just open the door and step out!

Tristan

P.S. Or is this more like Orpheus and Eurydice. Did you look back?

P.P.S Maybe there are certain conditions still unknown to us that are to be met if we are to *really* touch. And if not, our good-bye would then be the sharpest of blades through me.

Are souls formed in a spiritual vacuum yet engendered in the womb? Spontaneously condensed as an amalgam of cosmic strategies taking on earthly form? Are souls dreams turned inside out so that they can sensually encounter embodied things?

Writing to you now is like wading into a reservoir of sadness. I feel I've been taken to despair. I wish it weren't so. But this woe within me won't go away. You sought my soul, I believed. You gave me your heart, so I felt. Then without warning, your actions show how you'll never let me have it. Did you unwittingly predestine *this* conclusion all along? Doom yourself to face yourself, over and over?

Majnun who wanders in the Wasteland

P.S. Maybe someday you'll actually be given the kind of fruit you've been picking all this while.

If I could, I'd rewrite the current Kali Yuga's endgame.

Your smile is forever blossoming in my heart. "In every sacrifice there is the uncertainty of a journey toward an unknown destination." How do we know *how* to know? Real knowing is located both in the back and front of mind.

Yes, I still love you. And despite everything, I'm not afraid of it. I always said I would do what it takes. Are we at a place where being separate is unthinkable?

So yes. Come to me, I'll be here.

P.S. Everness, of course, is better than eternity because eternity is rather worn now. I used everness; but neverness is very beautiful though there is something hopeless about it, no? There is no word with the same meaning in any other language or in English. You might say impossibility, but that's not neverness. It's the Saxon ending *–ness*. Neverness. Keats uses nothingness: "Till love and fame to nothingness do sink"; but nothingness, I think, is weaker than neverness."   — Jorge Luis Borges

Does love when ripened develop into the crown of desiring?

As I love, I join the existences that gives birth to Time, Will, Wisdom. The angels of freshness exist in my blood, in my senses. Those angels speak to my higher self, their voices guide to me into the solution of us.

Tristan,
he of a tale of karma and Eros, of a romance excruciatingly intense
like a galaxy of explosions across the Universe

I remember the bodhisattva pendant I sent you long ago. How free it felt to give something so dear to me. And I remember how I've guarded much of myself, fearing losing you. Maybe not unlike someone trying to steal my god. I'm no longer burdened by the notion of you stealing my god. A god cannot be stolen. But can be happily given. And be happy to be a gift.

You've shown me an exposed god revealed in your letters; they have given me sanctuary. Ever since, I've lived by being loved and cherished by you. Clearly, I cannot be with anyone else.

Despite feeling wounded and resigned for a long time, I agree about what you mentioned, about my so-called secret life, the one you feel I have. In actuality it has to do with you. Longing for everything about you. My secret life is my faith. My faith's secret is: our karma is our wish.

Love,
Tristan

P.S. Nothing is ever lost, only transformed.

I just wrote a variation of my previous note. I'm addressing it to Heloise. You know, *that* Heloise.

I remember that first note I sent for your birthday along with the pendant, the one I was given by the monk Phar Wong. I gave what was so very close to me. Something I guarded deeply since the image of the bodhisattva was such deep comfort. Despite that, my lower self felt you were out to steal my god.

I was wrong. You stole my heart but not my god. Our god nurtures our higher aspirations. Now that we share the pendant, the bodhisattva carries us forward.

Peter

You don't need to be so careful with me. I mean, we already know lots of secrets about each other. Such intimacy. I know the pureness of your heart, and also know you're as naughty as can be. Thank God!

I realize that you imagine me entering you every morning. I've known since the moment you first wrote. You imagine me taking your fingers, lips into my mouth. Very slowly kissing you all over. You caress me stiff; place me in your mouth. With a fire that's relentless, I enter you every which way, over and over till, with drool and kisses and shouts you evaporate. Into untold bursts, we disappear as the walls shake, and the stars fall.

The ancient Egyptians believed our earthly deeds configured our true and genuine heart which was later weighed after death. Depending upon how the heart measured up to truth, love, honesty, and courage, passage into the Otherworld could progress. If it didn't, somebody would really be screwed.

Together we create fate, create our hearts. The consequences? That'll be assessed when our weighed hearts await review in the Otherworld.

Meanwhile...

QRST

I awaken to love as the beginning of the Cosmos once did. With an eye to the unknown, I awake to love as a disturbance without worries. I'm fused to love's wait, its mannerisms, its astral conducts, enthralling charge, imitations of animal existence. A tremendous satisfaction overtakes me. Lustrous, my cellular coherence roars. I'm at war with my solitude. I've destroyed my peace. I've unfastened myself feeling more and more as there's less and less of me.

I awaken to love intoxicated and ready. My mind a *before* and *after*, an *everness* right here steering me to itself.

I awaken to the seduction coursing through my blood. I've vandalized my serenity. All repose is disturbed. I've become a burglar stealing my own safety, casting it away. I'm an assassin introducing himself as the prey. I'm filled without understanding, casting aside propriety and cause. My past lies fallow as I awaken beyond boundaries. Drunk, sprawled, borderless, I stir like a teeming beehive, dancing to a sorcery devoid of ease. With the sting of passion what pierces me is no mere arrow, rather a violent spear puncturing a headless soul. I am loosed, plagiarizing every feeling, fornicating in the depths of thought, committing adultery with insensibility. Unhindered, I become a lightning flash, a fakir diving onto a bed of nails. My senses now metabolized, my viscera exploding.

I awaken to love here in my exquisite disturbance, burst open in the irrevocable paradise of you.

Tristan

Part 3

In essence, romantic understanding fosters inspiring
a universe of wisdom into a universe of love.

Toward Devotedness

Luminarias light the way for a plunge into the heart of possibility through the glow of love. A precious light radiating delight, and honeycomb, and innocence. Visibility at the edge of darkness, a sacrament for the night, tuned to the frequency of devotion.

In an atmosphere of casualness, 30,000 feet up in the sky, they meet: an improbable chance encounter. Settled in the window seat next to him, he hands off the drink to her offered by the flight attendant. She thanks him then coyly asks about the unusual text he's reading. During the flight, exchanges of niceties develop into profound soul admissions, and affinities. Upon landing, they bid each other farewell; in a more or less formal gesture they exchanging addresses. It's improbable they'd ever see each other again. They live two thousand miles apart. However, again initiated by her, they, over a seven-year period write steadily to each other, revealing the depth of their feelings and the aspirations of their evolving hearts. She has a husband; he has a lover; nevertheless, they fall deeply in love. Little outwardly happens till her indecisions and his exasperation can no longer sustain the vision. That is, till she makes a move. Ostensibly free, they make an attempt to realize their dreams. They fathom that their love has the potential for articulating the physiology of their karma, to realize the vocation of their souls; their sublime lineaments seeking to voice creation itself through romance, ardor, and ultimately physical union. Throughout their joined destiny they portray the joys and pitfalls of longing, romance, fantasy, love at a distance, and spiritual transcendence. From the very center of their hearts, they ask: Did our devotion to one another shape the mysterious world in which we exist? Did our disclosures and trials mean something more significant than just personally for us? Did our love *have to* be?

Corresponding Hinges of Soul

Of those little coincidences that no longer astound her: the day before his letter arrived she began reading Augustine's *Confessions*. And yet, little coincidences do astound her. The very same day, he read about Shelley's "desire of the moth for the star."

Startled for no apparent reason, she reached for the door seconds before the doorbell rang. Her heart beat in pure excitement with the turn of the knob. There on the stoop was a package, a gift from him. Red tulips! Her world slung wide open. That same instant, on another continent across the Atlantic, he opened an envelope. It was the color of springtime blushing. Opening the letter, she had kissed the paper inside, pressing its surface deeply with the redness of her lips.

Sex for the adoring soul was a corporeal metaphor for spiritual love, he had written to her. In ancient Egypt the hieroglyph for love shows a man with his hand to his mouth, sometimes the hand is in his mouth. Alone at home, nearly every morning for the seven years prior to their second meeting, she first placed her hand in her mouth, then slowly under the covers opened her thighs, touching herself while her soul drank him in.

The Heart of Future Into Past

Replying to her query regarding who enjoys sex more, a man or a woman, the goddess Hera struck Tiresias—advisor to Cadmus the founder and king of Thebes—blind. Why her anger? And, why the curse when Tiresias claims there's no contest: a woman's pleasure is ten times greater than a man's? Hera's husband Zeus's subsequently recompenses Tiresias by giving him the gift of clairvoyance together with seven additional lifetimes. For Zeus, who appears to act on something resembling a cosmic principle of recompense, existence is held in the balance of enormous forces some of which he can affect; his is a gift dispensed with irony, as if to say, "I endow you with foresight since you should have kept your mouth shut." From Hera's perspective, Tiresias's answer, while perhaps accurate, was immoderately blunt. It would have been far more appropriate had he said, "Certain women enjoy sex far more under specific circumstances such as when pleasuring themselves, or in the company of a sensitive, knowledgeable lover." Without those conditions his answer suggests a woman idolizes the sex act, receiving immoderately more than her male counterpart; possibly more than her gender is due.

132

The spite of the Greek gods recurs most during squabbles about sex. However the story of Tiresias harbors a twist. Bear in mind, the main theme concerns Hera, one of the pantheon of Olympians who in many respects lacks clear conscience and morality; and Tiresias, son a mortal shepherd become advisor. Owing to his lineage—his mother was a Nymph—he is destined to become a prophet of Apollo, the sun god. A deeper look into the history of this story discovers that Tiresias' transgression was originally founded upon him at one time interrupting two snakes while they were copulating, a significant event from a nature-ritual perspective. He effectively acted contrary to the natural order with regard to the snakes' instincts, then guilelessly assessed libidinal experience from his belief and perspective. Hera though is the variety of goddess who feels Tiresias' answer is in fact true yet she's incensed that anyone less than a god would be so audacious to voice it. From her point of view his audacity was a transgression for which he had to pay.

For ancient seers, the physical body was considered as having one gender; the complementary soul harboring the other gender. In other words, Tiresias was first a male body with a female soul then became female with a male soul. This suggests that his understanding of Hera's query comes from his entire being, not merely his gender. For a accurate understanding of reality something beyond appearances is needed: the recognition that the soul and body are in a conversation choreographed through multiple lifetimes. Present sensation may give rise to later insights. Fixations now may beget variability another time. This notion isn't meant to paint a portrait of androgyny or hermaphroditism, rather a hierogamy, a holy union, an alchemical marriage of the forces within one and all conveying possibilities through circumstances of feeling and flesh. Sex as a sensual, profound act is only possible in the kinds of bodies we have. And with the sorts of souls that elucidate the dynamics of sense experience. The history of the human condition demonstrates this reality.

As to the question of who enjoys sex more: it's ultimately a mute point especially since sex cannot be defined solely by corporeal pleasure, though the simplicity of the myth's customary account might have us think so. Hera upholds the underlying principle of natural law. In spite of this, she grows incensed when the subject is laid out in the open. With swift justice, a disingenuous modesty rears its head through her impetuous fury. This, from the sole goddess ever depicted through artistic imagery as placing her mouth amorously around Zeus's erect phallus. Zeus on the other hand is at times insatiable, seizing anything and anyone he desires. Yet with Tiresias, his ephemeral lustiness capitulates to a developed sensibility. Zeus bestows a warranted redress, conscience-like. The spirit's logic holds true even if inside out.

For the modern psyche, the larger concern lies in the imagination of personal experience. What lives in the future meets the endeavors of today, whereas what brings us to this day is the longing we have for the future. The sense world and our histories and experiences exist with our anticipations of the yet-to-be; and these alongside our moods concerning the unknown. We can be quite preoccupied with the future when asleep to some many things. Soulful presence asks us to address how urges themselves may have a relentless need to blossom, no matter what. And how desire, conscience, sensitivity and imagination each play their significant role for our existence. With regard to the beloved, or the lusted-for, there's the the question of why we expose and bear each other's yearning, whether through the wish for sensual fruition, emotional play, tactile fusion, or transcendence. Concerning this, each of us activates our own occasion of prophecy while scarcely knowing *what* it is we really want, and what is our wanting's genuine purpose. And do we aspire to develop the ability to deal with it all.

Yearning Is the Nerve of Love

Romanticism regards yearning as the impulse amplifying boundaries of the ordinary. Novalis' "unquenchable thirst" and Kierkegaard's "love as a wound" reference desire as the antecedent of love's pathway. Denis De Rougemont's analysis in *Love In the Western World* views passion and sexual responsiveness as a kind of participation in mystical grace. Mario Praz's *The Romantic Agony* delves into the darker roots of erotic sensibility; how the history of moribund fascinations, decadence and "luxurious cruelties" have influenced literature and art, especially how their nightmarish obsessions take up residence in the psyche. Julius Evola's *Metaphysics of Sex* set out to elucidate how the archetypes of sexual force lead to transcendence and redemption, or destruction and annihilation through the potent power of erotic allure. Other

134

approaches regard desire as a relentlessly mysterious force engaging the sensual toward some prospective satisfaction even if incomplete or vague.

Orthodox dogmas cast sensuality as a protagonist reinforcing the sense world, separating the soul from divine will. The effects of the sensual realm became an underlying source for a great deal of religious morality. The post Eden predicament of *being seen* supports the context of a "higher" realm whose province defines certain moral ideals. Failure to comply results in moral judgments resulting in guilt and shame. The fundamental issue involves resisting a force that imbues life with the desire for union with the object of attraction. One such force is Eros, the god of intimate love and pursuer of Psych. Eros exploits the mortal realm by heightening longing, extolling attraction; he infuses the soul's carnality, urging desire to act out with a goal in mind. Union with that which bestows pleasure, euphoria, and bliss. With regard to Nature on the whole, action is instinctual, and resolves for the sake of sexual reproduction. For humankind there is of course much more.

A great deal came about with regard to the religious and philosophical duality between the intellect and the senses, between chaos and order. A route through the exigencies of will, a timeless play of contrasting tendencies, ventures into the urgently physical or the transcendent. Does the sensual defile the spirit? If so, why was the sense world created in the first place? Does the spiritual in some way *need* the sense world in order to be complete in physical setting? If so, the spirit must be deficient in some way. Spiritually, does love employ attraction to activate the senses toward a higher purpose? Is the human being bound in some struggle for validating feelings, only then resist them? Sensually, does "spirit" exist as the operative director guiding reproductive urge? Are lust and pleasure agencies for evolution? Though religion generally represses Eros' tactics, while often concealing its fascination with his backsides. The above questions present cognitive dilemmas when facing the subject at hand.

The phenomenologist Maurice Merleau-Ponty points out that in the act of perception there is no experience of sensation. *Seeing* is unencumbered by the mechanics of *how* we see. *Hearing* is an experience is an experience we have yet we've no idea of what is actually happening within the ear, nerves, and brain. Engaging the senses, we are free *to* sense yet bound to those workings in which we do not consciously participate. We have no experience of sensation while perceiving. Similarly with desire, we experience longing apart from understanding what occurs in the desiring moment. We feel attraction; we grow passionate. The process develops right through our biological development as the psyche is triggered and feelings heighten. Seeing or simply imagining the beloved can summon Eros' arrow.

And yet, something deeper can be discerned: the *motives* within attraction. Attraction positions Eros' demanding force; he acts through that which exists by way of the agreeable, the alluring, or the pheromonal draw. These enervations are his means of powering longing. By way of desire, Eros urges the soul to reposition ordinary consciousness. Life is markedly beholden to his influence and much that ensues is the consequence of yielding to him. Sublime or explicit, detectable or invisible, Eros is strung through the senses, conveying his influence with an intensity that may go so far as to exhaust life itself.

Eros, as most accounts portray him, is the son of Aphrodite, goddess of love and beauty. He's a mischievous rogue facilitating attraction and the bonds of love to form, sometimes illicitly intercourse between gods and humans. Though later satirical poets represent him as a blindfolded child—the capricious Cupid—in early Greek poetry he was depicted as an adult male embodying raw, elemental sexual power. As Apuleius narrates in *The Golden Ass*, Eros inadvertently sticks himself with his own dart of desire, becoming enchanted with his mother's sister, Psyche—the personification of soul—taken with her unparalleled mortal beauty. To illustrate her worthiness and redeem the injurious effects of her sisters' betrayal, Eros' mother, Aphrodite, mounts a number of severe trails for Psyche. Though Aphrodite herself was resentful of Psyche's effects on her son, Psyche prevails with the aid of the supernatural world. Eros and Psyche eventually reunite once Psyche becomes immortal. The daughter of their union is none other than Pleasure, Bliss. The attraction between Eros and Psyche renders a mythic prototype for human trials of romantic involvement. Through the piercing of stunned souls, the seizing of desire labors to survive discouragement despite immense obstacles. Cunning, calamity, craving, conjugal relations and the horizon of death merge into a inexorable rite of passage, a transition that, for some, will be designated "heaven," or "happiness." Despite all this, Psyche braves life's maze when the spirit realm adopts soulful compassion, reaching for the higher objective of love, Love itself full of care and concern.

136

Unraveling attraction, we come to Eros' character reaching much further than the pursuer of Psyche. Eros is everywhere we come to realize, all through the commencement of impulse. In the deep abyss before earthly existence, love's desire out from depths of darkness and night was like a bird who took to wing in the form of the *who* who existed before self, the *who* who established self and objective otherness. This otherness was none other than the archetypal human who was, in effect, the supreme object of divine love. In the most ancient of myths, mind hadn't a clue about how to think; mind was *ardor*. Only afterward did ardor bifurcate into *being*. When we hear Aristophanes recount primordial evolution he means to go well beyond the notions of passions and pangs:

"At the beginning there was only Chaos (Kaos), Night (Nyx), Darkness (Erebus), and the Abyss (Tartarus). Earth, the Air and Heaven had no existence. Firstly, black-winged Night laid a germless egg in the bosom of the infinite deeps of Darkness, and from this, after the revolution of long ages, sprang the graceful Love (Eros) with his glittering golden wings, swift as the whirlwinds of the tempest. He mated in the deep Abyss with dark Chaos, winged like himself, and thus hatched forth our race, which was the first to see the light."

As longing saturates the soul, Eros suffuses throughout the feeling life. To the observant soul it's clear that feeling cannot be annulled. But it can indeed be recognized. Eros lives through the forces of feeling for the desired; he offers himself as a gift. Eros facilitates the urgency to the object of attraction. He breathes desire like an emanation of primal will. If he is to be understood, it's with an imaginative faculty picturing and contemplating his impulse. Though will force within yeaning itself is nigh impossible to consciously grasp, it can be met by attempting to unravel the allure-laden circumstance *backwards*.

Unraveling the mysterious power of Eros, the soul can recognize what desire employs as its foremost means: attraction. And what it sets out to achieve: satisfaction. Both are fermented by allure, invigorated through romance. Attraction renews Eros' own imagination. By meeting the force of his desire both ecstatically *and* consciously, yearning is recognized and accomplished. Even if the point of Eros' aim faces the possibility of annihilation, his arrow penetrates as the principle of attraction. The pleasure of yearning towards satisfaction is not unlike the death impulse, the release from the physical world. Satisfaction is its destiny, the aim of desire. Desire was necessary imparted before *anything* could begin, for existence to manifest, for the necessity of time and existential context. Desire ever since its inception needed to be directed. else yearning couldn't steer toward an objective. As the beloved is positioned at the center of meaning—the point of utter attractiveness—physical attraction and its sensual fulfillment may be the dominant urge. In contrast, a spiritual connection devoid of carnal relations may take attraction to a higher ideal. Whichever the pathway, eroticism cannot be defined by fixed criteria or by excluding the possibility of yearning. Love is directed to the *subject* of love. Sensuality as such expresses the coherence between sense, soul, and spirit. Within attraction is the concealed search for the depth of feeling itself. Without direction, attraction devolves viscerally into sheer will, suffusing into an insensible domain fomenting self-absorption, vanity, and mere physical gratification; conditions manifesting misshapen degrees of pleasure. The unaffected goal—satisfaction, however equivocal—wishes to be realized throughout soul, spirit and body.

The primal impulse embedded throughout life and death arose before life and death were separate. Through longing, the world came to be our of a cosmologic act, the emanation of spirit into body, ensoulment bearing the course. Through this development, the senses assemble, each apprehending a portion of the world, enabling a framework for comprehending the whole. Sensation without this understanding remains unfocused, directionless. What could exist as merely compulsive can and ought to blossom into moral perception for the aspiring human being. Meeting this idea, the desirous soul's faculty endures and modulates Eros' conduct, directing its power toward the feeling of love.

Without a finger on longing's pulse, the soul is subject to undisciplined yearning, an kind of emissary of Eros, apt to undertake urgency whichever way fate takes it. Romance shapes the lineaments of longing, proposing the subjectivity and objectivity of desiring. Romanticism thus requires an understanding of capacities and potential failures, all marks of awakened sensibility and conscientious knowing. Given a sense of bearing, romantic sensibility conveys devotion while exalting the value of the other. The value of what's invested in another being can never take away from the value of what it *means* to devote oneself in the most genuine ways possible. The course

138

of sensation accordingly receives its force back into itself while liberated toward the conscious aptitude to love. This is a free act unfettering the perceivable from the fixed, from the reactive and obsessive. Moreover, its effort emancipates the subconscious' tendencies to posses the other, paving the way for the spirit to fructify desire by fostering morality not out of a prescribed imperative but out of the free deed of conscious action embracing difficulties and joys. Moral development serves to satisfy the soul's yearning throughout spirit *and* self.

Facing Eros, the Romantic poet William Blake affirmed, "The lust of the goat is the bounty of God." Yes, and desire made transparent delivers the longing and unfinished state of Eros' effort back to Eros himself, freeing the god who so desperately desires us to yearn

Metempsychoses and an Affaire de Cœur

The god of ritual madness in ancient Greece, Dionysus was as well the god of ecstasy, liberator from self-conscious fear, and repression. The 19th century philosopher, Friedrich Nietzsche, a self-proclaimed disciple of Dionysius, in his unique way shook culture, and the meaning of human endeavor, expanded how their roles are responsible for shouldering the evolution of individuality. Working to overcome the pessimism of Arthur Schopenhauer and the "small-spiritedness" of the English philosophers (especially the "utility" framework of Mill), and the demeaning dogmas of prevailing Christianity, Nietzsche not only fought for freedom from prejudice and outmoded morals, his soul cried out in a wilderness of superficiality and intellectual deceit. Interestingly, Nietzsche held a number of American authors dear, among them Mark Twain, Edgar Allan Poe and, above all, Ralph Waldo Emerson. Nietzsche considered the perceptive and insightful Emerson "a twin soul."

A chronicler of Friedrich Nietzsche's inner life might imagine the philosopher, upon reading Emerson, taken into an inestimably elated state of ardor. Throughout Emerson's major motifs one can recognize Nietzsche's own ideas regarding the will to power, destiny, loving one's fate, how desires and drives are converted into traits and consequences, the ideal of the over-man, and more. By 1882, after abandoning his relationship with most colleagues, then splitting with the assessments of the later Romantic German composer Richard Wagner, Nietzsche had few remaining friends. To boot, the alienating style and attitude towards Christianity displayed throughout his *Thus Spoke Zarathustra* guaranteed Nietzsche would be unemployable in a university setting. Nietzsche's response was to become more solitary. His writings largely ignored, in 1885 he printed only 40 copies of part four of *Zarathustra*, distributing only a fraction of these among close allies. In 1886 Nietzsche self-published *Beyond Good and Evil*, in which he expounds on the "new philosophers" whose imagination, self-assertion, danger, originality and "creating of values" could lead the modern soul into uncharted territory. Burdened with chronic digestive problems, insomnia, and headaches, Nietzsche was consistently self-medicating with sedatives and digestives. Then on January 3rd 1889 Nietzsche suffered a complete mental breakdown. The precise facts of what happened remain unknown, but shortly after his collapse more than a few accounts claim that Nietzsche witnessed the flogging of a horse across the Piazza Carlo Alberto in Turin, Italy. He ran to the horse, threw his arms up around its neck in attempt to protect it. He next folded to the ground into a psychotic stare, his mind and life irrevocably altered from that moment on.

• • •

An introverted sort, mostly unknown and unpublished in her time, Emily Dickinson was destined to become one of the most important among American poets. Dickinson spent most of her life in Amherst, Massachusetts in almost complete isolation, yet she maintained active correspondences with her closest friends the whole while. She was considered an inspiration to her nieces, nephews, and the neighborhood children, and was regarded fondly by her respectful siblings, Austin and Lavinia. With percipient zeal she eagerly read Longfellow, Wordsworth, Shakespeare, John Keats and Walt Whitman while maintaining her splendid flower garden. It's told that Emily attended a lecture by Ralph Waldo Emerson; the orator spent an evening at her neighbor's abode the very night of his presentation. Emily however was too shy to speak with him in person. In 1866, after a number of friends and family had died, Emily's curly-coated Newfoundland, Carlo, passed away as well. After providing a gentle, protective canine presence for over sixteen years, Carlo's departure set off a deep melancholy in Emily. Her poems after that largely reflected on death and immortality, inquiries regarding the self and the landscape of the spirit. Known to the local villagers as the "lady in white," she was only ever spotted wearing white dresses. By and by, Emily ceased to speak to visitors face-to-face, engaging them only from the inside of her front door. Emily's emotional depth runs much further than the dramatic characterization of her literary mentor, Thomas Wentworth Higginson. Higginson was a Bostonian literary critic, a radical slavery abolitionist, a women's rights proponent and former Unitarian minister. To him she wrote, "I am small, like the wren, and my hair is bold, like the chestnut bur, and my eyes like the sherry in the glass that the guest leaves." But when Higginson finally visited Emily in Amherst in 1870 he candidly felt he never was "with any one who drained my nerve power so much. Without touching her, she drew [all force] from me..." Later he picked up the thread, "The bee himself did not evade the schoolboy more than she evaded me, and even at this day I still stand somewhat bewildered, like the boy." Emily manifested traits spiritually strange and unapproachable, only to promptly turn coy or flirty; she embodied contradiction wrapped in layers of self-awareness and nuance. Upon her death it was discovered that she had written nearly eighteen hundred poems and, though most of her letters had been burned, nearly a thousand survived. Puzzling, dazzling and allusive, highly sensitive and attuned to her receivers' moods and proclivities, Emily was eventually hailed as a most prolific observer of self and persona, an explorer of attentiveness, passion and sensitivity; a poet who engaged the span of tenderness' mysteries.

● ● ●

Emily Dickinson (1830–1886) and Friedrich Nietzsche (1844–1900). Born fourteen years apart, each lived to be 55 years old. Both engaged in a unique transcendence well before their death. One can imagine Friedrich's and Emily's subtle souls in the afterlife plausibly searching; their distilled longing toward a higher satisfaction, so robust. That they might pursue the spirit of one another remains of course mere speculation even the most gracious theosophists might opine. Yet, sustained outside their yearning-filled isolation, *that* they *would* deeply seek one another ought to be unmistakably, heartbreakingly clear.

Dimension and Participation

Love relationships are habitually defined by the template of duality. It's been said that love is the overcoming of the self through the other, an unwitting strategy for transcendence. One's hope is that the beloved, the *other*, can really see us. Liberation through recognition. In this scenario exist tremendous forces of expectation and polarization that are capable of pulling relationships apart. Relationships in modern times have become extraordinarily difficult. The need for personal autonomy alongside the reservoir of undigested past experiences, unplumbed spirit and psyche, dysfunctional fantasy, and lack of genuine community are just a few reasons. In contrast, there is a tremendous force to be gained with regard to relationship if a triadic paradigm is introduced: two *plus* a fulcrum capable of mirroring individuality's recklessness and reason, its pains and aspirations. Introducing a spiritual fulcrum into a relationship allows love to create its own environment. Inside love's dynamism, those in relationship are enabled to become clearer viewers, adept listeners. Effectively, a relationship's dangers and risks, flaws and potentials, stand to gain room to breathe. The treasure of one's otherness is open to identifying the shocking power of love and romance, recognizing being in the throes of impulsiveness, practical difficulties, and egotism. This fulcrum may be imagined as that borne upon history, disappointment, betrayal, rage, hurt, sadness, God, or fate. What the fulcrum consists of is not the primary point in the relational *quality* of relationship; it simply admits to recognizing that we mostly don't know how to *do* love. In reality, we harbor a capacity to go so far as to wish to destroy the other due to this very failure on our part. Despite the fact that direct apprehension of the soul of another is not in our normal conscious domain, our feeling life can in fact embrace the soul qualities displayed before us. The soul of another *is* palpable nonetheless, from an altogether novel approach cognizing what brought us to the beloved in the first place. For this we must qualify the very context of the fulcrum: the World-Soul, the world itself. Exercising this wisdom-laden "lever" can, with proper intention, lead to a sound understanding of what endangers and disrupts the meaning and harmony of relationship. Goethe assertion, "the eternal feminine lures to perfection" implicates the destiny of longing and wholeness. The structure of "romance," an axis beyond dyad to triad, includes personal pathos, expectations and existential longings, as well as the reflective force acting through the conditions and possibilities for learning. In this light, we gaze upon the future of human experience as not just individual experience: love beyond the mirror of our selves. The *how* of this fulcrum is the vitally cognized and acted upon dimension of romance which pierces through psychic muddle, enjoying the presence of what is god-like and child-like in the other, the beloved. This, while educating sensuality to become a force for the wholeness of the world. There is no precedent for this. It needs to be invented, to engage the will and exercise the imagination beyond self-absorption. To journey through and beyond, one must have faith in the mission of selfhood.. The world in countless significant ways is asking for humanity to come of age. Through love. Through us.

Sanctity and Wish

She instigated the whole thing. He instigated the whole thing. In spirit and ache they pursued one another. Beyond overwhelming odds their feelings prevailed. Straining interpretation, memory and orientation, they became each other's thread, a thread on which loving could be strung, revealing what canceled those loves from before, disclosing what hadn't *been*. Through this thread a resonance flowed through their desires and aspirations, sustaining a path for exalting the dream of their togetherness. Together, they witnessed seven years of their lives stretched across the breadth of the mesa, reflecting: how could there be such connection? Such determination?

• • •

Looking for visible signs for the origin of the Cosmos, astronomers say that the farther we look the deeper into the past we see. It can be inferred that the future looks back to the beginning, dreams from the future promoting our desires and wishes. Is the horizon of togetherness a perennially expanding dimension? Does our longing for love grow ever larger?

• • •

As light lengthens, outside, the cicadas begin their song. Stirred by dreams, lifeblood and closed eyes, tongues moisten. Lips ready. A wave begins its glide across their faces. In their very core the aptitude of mystery avows to greet the new morning.

"Seeking the mother tongue of the deepest self, shall we sing of a bird? The wind? The desert? Of life assembling us?"

"Esta es e el corazón, el alma, la comprensión. Esto es nuestra poesía, nace del deseo. We are wet and wetness does not keep its form. Through our hearts we echo ahead of any storm. We kiss, we become fire, and are freed by our hunger."

Inspired with blessings, they press on in time as the world stills, listens, seeks them as its flame, its essence, its darling radiation. By means of their hearts they reach: What is it to set free the soul's horizon? What is it to be baptized in the name of your wishes?

QBSP

Andrew Franck's writings include *The Transparent Bride*, *The Art of Porosity*, *Mantras and Musical Solutions*, *The Holy Bodies Circuit*, and *The Painted Trout*

andrewfranck.net

Archetextural
archetextural@gmail.com

Woodstock NY 12498